BEATING THE ODDS OF MARCH

Winning Betting Strategies
for the
2025 NCAA Basketball Tournament

By: Alan B. Sheats

DISCLAIMER

While the author and publisher used their best efforts to accurately prepare this book, they make no warranties with respect to accuracy or completeness of its contents. Further, the author and the publisher specifically disclaim any implied warranty of merchantability or fitness for a particular purpose. No warranty may be created or extended by a sales representative or written sales materials.

The general advice and strategies discussed in this book may not be suitable to your particular situation. Further, this book does not provide any advice on the legality of any wager with respect to state or federal law.

Neither the author nor the publisher will be liable for any loss claimed on account of this book including but not limited to profits as well as consequential, incidental, or punitive damages.

2025 Edition
Editor   Linda Lupco
Cover Design   Alan Sheats
Proofreading   Linda Lupco
Printing   Amazon Direct
ISBN:
Paperback   979-8-3005546-4-4
Hardcover   979-8-3005580-3-1

Alan Sheats
Beating the Odds of March Winning Betting Strategies for the 2025 NCAA Basketball Tournament/ Alan Sheats: edited by Linda Lupco
Pages: 21 cm x 29.5 cm

ACKNOWLEDGEMENT

Very special thanks to Linda Lupco for her indispensable assistance in
the creation of this book.

DEDICATION

This book is dedicated to the past glory of the original Pac-12 Conference that ended its final season as an association in 2024. The Conference is immortalized with six different institutions contributing to sixteen national Division 1 Men's Basketball Championships. The Pac-12 has also long been the crucible for legions of college and professional stars and legends of the game.

Sadly, the original Pac-12 is no more but its rich history and fond memories will indelibly endure.

To bet or
not to bet-that
is the question

Inspired by
William Shakespeare

TABLE OF CONTENTS

2025 TOURNAMENT SCHEDULE

Selection Sunday: Sunday, March 16

First Four: Tuesday, March 18; Wednesday, March 19

First Round: Thursday, March 20; Friday, March 21

Second Round: Saturday, March 22; Sunday, March 23

Third Round: Thursday, March 27; Friday, March 28

Fourth Round: Saturday, March 28; Sunday, March 29

Fifth Round: Saturday, April 5

Championship Game: Monday, April 7

INTRODUCTION

The main mission of Beating the Odds of March is to furnish direction for betting on the 2025 NCAA Division 1 Men's Basketball "Tournament," also called "The Big Dance" or "Dance." More particularly, this guidance ranges from providing a novel, better, and faster way of assembling a Tournament bracket to supplying gambling strategies that can be selected in line with the gambler's personal style to identify profitable betting options.

Betting goals of this book are pursued by using strategies that partially embrace Lady Luck all the way to considering the science of statistics. This is to enlighten the gambling decisions of everyone from the casual bettor to the advanced gambler. In any event, the twenty-day spectacle that is the Tournament is arguably the most unique wagering opportunity on the sports calendar.

Wagering on the Tournament is distinguished from most other sports wagering because it is informed by two authoritative sources, the NCAA Committee and actual betting odds generated from the consensus of influential sportsbooks. It is this "double vetting" arrangement whereby the NCAA Committee intentionally arranges mismatches of teams, which sportsbooks later quantify with their initial posting of odds, that makes Tournament betting special. However, to make money, strategy and luck still need to come together.

To that end, the book endeavors to educate the gambler about betting on college basketball in general and serve as a self-help workbook that can be written in or, more appropriately, should be described as a "win book" for beating the odds of March in 2025 (See the Tournament schedule opposite page). The book has frequent references to the 2022, 2023, and 2024. Tournaments. This is because while the invited teams and players change, the concepts discussed here, as shown by the analysis of recent Tournament history, are expected to endure and certainly be relevant to better predict winning bets during the 2025 Championship.

The unmatched gambling opportunities of the Tournament are combined with unparalleled excitement, delivering on the promise of unbelievable plays and edge-of-your-seat buzzer-beaters. Moreover, these thrills can be taken to another level by going beyond mundane betting on a cell phone to all-in with an actual trip to a sportsbook. This is particularly true if that destination is the likes of Atlantic City, Las Vegas, or Reno. With such a trip when the games are in recess, there is access to the casinos (don't lose your Tournament stake), shows, great restaurants, and clubs. However, a mix of business and pleasure is tempered by the reality that successful Tournament betting will almost certainly require considerable effort, which is fortunately streamlined by this book.

Simplifying the analysis of proposed bets is extremely helpful to the gambler, especially because the lion's share of Tournament gambling opportunities are compressed in the first two rounds of the Championship, featuring 48 of its 67 total contests. It is on these four days that the biggest mismatches present themselves, and the most money is on the table for the taking.

The following pages describe betting terminology, wagering strategies, tables, charts, various examples of bets, and novel betting forms. All of this is calculated to improve the likelihood that wagering on the Tournament will be skill-driven and fortunate enough to beat the odds of March.

BASIC BETTING TERMINOLOGY

- The **House**—administers the wagering. This includes setting the "odds" (defined below), printing those odds on bet sheets, accepting bets, printing the bet tickets, and paying for winning Tickets. The House makes money by setting up wagering scenarios such that it takes in more money in bets than it pays out in winning tickets. The funds received by the House for organizing the betting are called the "juice."

- The **favorite**—is the team expected to win a game, according to the House.

- The **dog** (short for underdog)—is the team expected to lose a game, according to the House.

- **Odds**—are the probability that something will happen. On a wager, odds reflect the amount of a wager required to win $100 using positive and negative numbers. A negative number is assigned to a bet requiring more than $100 to win $100, and a positive number shows how much more than $100 is paid on a $100 bet. Therefore, -115 odds signal that a bet of $115 is required to win $100. If a $100 bet is made on an event with +105 odds, a winning Ticket pays $105. When the odds are listed by the House as "EV," this is shorthand for even. With these odds, a $100 bet has a payout of $100.

- An **opening line**—is the initial odds for a bet set by the House intended to get equal action from gamblers on both sides of a wagering opportunity. Once an opening line is established, these numbers change before a contest begins according to how gamblers actually place their money (See odds above).

- The **spread** (short for point spread)—is the number of points either subtracted from the favorite or added to the dog that the favorite must win by or the dog cannot lose by to win the game for the purpose of the bet ticket. For instance, a favorite team that has a -7 spread has to win by at least 8 points to win on a bet ticket. Correspondingly, a dog with a +7-point spread can lose by as much as 6 points and still win the bet. Naturally, a team that is a dog is also a winner if they upset the favorite on the court by winning the game.

- The **money line**—is a bet that the chosen team will win. The favorite and dog groups are differentiated by the assignment of odds. The favored team has a payoff that is calculated by a formula intended to pay a smaller portion of the amount bet as the likelihood of a win increases. For example, if the favorite has a -400 money line, a $10 bet pays $2.50 to win (25%). If the money line on this favorite increases to -800, the payment on a $10 bet shrinks to only $1.25 (12.5%).

  Conversely, as the probability of a dog losing increases, the gambler is enticed to wager on them by offering a larger payoff. If a dog has a +400 money line and wins, a bet of $10 pays $40 (400%). But if the money line for that dog escalates to +800, the $10 bet is worth $80 (800%) for a win.

- The **over**—is a bet that the total points scored by both teams, called the "Total," will be above a number established by the House for a selected portion of the game. This is typically the entire game or at halftime.

- The **under**—is a bet that the total points scored by both teams will be below a number established by the House for a selected portion of the game, which is typically the entire game or at halftime.

- A **parlay**—is a wager on two or more outcomes on the same bet Ticket. Each contest used in a parlay is referred to as a "leg," all of which must be won or result in a "push" (see below) to collect on the ticket. The attraction of a parlay is that as more legs are added to the ticket, a small wager can be converted into a potentially sizable payout. However, the likelihood of winning multiple outcomes is low. It's hard enough to win one contest!

- **Covering**—means the gambler meets the requirements of a spread, making them eligible to collect money from the House. Thus, if a team that is +8 on the spread loses by 6 points, the dog team has covered the spread and is the winner for the purpose of betting. Conversely, if a team is favored, having a -8 point spread, and "wins" by 7 points, for betting purposes, the wager is a loser.

- A **push**—describes an individual bet or a leg of a parlay where the actual outcome of the game is the same number as the number on the ticket that determines a win or a loss. For example, in a $10 bet for a team with a spread of -7, if that team wins by seven, the gambler only gets their $10 back. A push would also result in an over or under bet on a Total of 135 for the complete-game, where the final combined score of the teams is actually 135. With a parlay bet, if a leg of the parlay pushes and the other legs win, the card is paid as a parlay with one less leg. Therefore, a three-team parlay with a leg that is a push and two legs that win is paid as a two-leg parlay.

- **First-half** betting—means the betting options of the spread, money line, and Total can be wagered for the first half of a game (See www.betql.co/ncaab/odds/first-half.com). This means that in college basketball, you will know if you have won the wager after only 20 minutes of play. A half-time bet eliminates the prospect of overtime and can avoid the drawn-out drama of the end of games marked by time-outs and fouling that can extend the end of a contest with only seconds left to several minutes of gambler's anguish.

- A **bet payout**—is the profit that the gambler receives over and above the amount of a wager for a winning ticket. As a case in point, for a $10 bet at -110 odds, the payout for winning is $9.09, with the gambler getting back a total of $19.09.

- The term "**Chalk**" bet—for the purposes of this book, is a money line bet for the complete-game or, at halftime, on a favorite team. A chalk bet is a prediction that there is not going to be any upset in the game being wagered on. The problem is that heavy favorites with large negative money line numbers do lose, and even when they win, the payout is small (See odds above).

INITIAL BETTING CONSIDERATIONS

FAMILIARITY WITH TOURNAMENT TEAMS

Betting on the Tournament can be aided by having some knowledge about participating teams. This knowledge may be acquired in many ways, including actually watching games during the college basketball season to form your own subjective evaluation of squads, the "eye test." Information about teams may also be gained from secondary sources such as:
- Reading sports articles and blogs concerning college basketball;
- Watching sports television programs about college basketball;
- Examining college basketball statistics;
- Tracking college basketball ranking sources, and:
- Monitoring conference basketball tournaments at the end of the regular season.

With respect to statistics in evaluating college basketball teams, care should be taken. The main reason for this is that the actions of teams are not like a random coin toss, the meat and potatoes of statistical analysis. The outcomes of games are biased events and, as such, can derail an attempt to predict them in a classic statistical fashion. One manifestation of this bias is that teams frequently change their character during the course of the season.

At the beginning of the season, teams often have not established their "identity," including a selection of starting personnel, interaction of players (gelling), and style of play. Additionally, the reliability of statistics can become questionable because teams are unlikely to play the same level of competition at the same time of year. Some teams have been forged by battling with heavyweight challengers, while others have feasted on "creampuff" opponents, padding statistics to the point of them being grossly misleading.

Moreover, putting too much stock in early season games can be a problem with marginal teams that may have pulled off a major upset because the defeated, high-profile team may simply not be playing up to their potential when these games are contested. Teams that are really not that good can get a signature win or two early in the season, cruise through a weak conference, and compile an impressive numerical resume. But remember, it's who and when you play as well as how many games you win. Despite inherent limitations, college basketball statistics are available from several internet sources, including www.teamrankings.com and www.cbbanalytics.com.

This book contemplates but does not guarantee access to some statistical scoring data for the regular season for each of the 68 teams in the Tournament through a gamblers' request to the book's email beatingtheoddsofmarch@yahoo.com. This information allows a comparison of game opponents on various scoring dimensions that relate to wagering strategies outlined in this book (See an example of a statistical comparison of teams on pages 53 and 54). The scoring data on all 68 Tournament teams is expected to be available shortly after Selection Sunday.

The scoring data forms described above are only for games during the regular season. Conference tournament results are not provided because it is believed that teams have too many ulterior motives in these contests, making statistical analysis untrustworthy.

With respect to betting in consideration of team rankings, periodic review of college basketball polls can be a replacement for other information sources (except for conference tournaments contested after the final Poll) about college basketball teams and, in particular, lessen the need for a deep statistical dive into those teams. These polls start in earnest several weeks into the regular season, usually coming out every Monday once this process starts. At a minimum, college basketball polls identify a significant number of teams that are likely to be in the Tournament.

By keeping track of the twenty-five teams in the polls as well as the approximate ten teams that are in the polls at some time but drop below the twenty-five-team threshold, the gambler is made aware of approximately thirty-five teams that will almost certainly make the Tournament. This awareness is helpful because after Selection Sunday on March 16, 2025, you only have one day before the preliminary Tournament starts on Tuesday and just three days prior to the beginning of the First Round of the Tournament starting at 9:00 am on Thursday, March 18, 2025, to examine the field for first-round wagering opportunities (See Tournament Rounds, page 11).

As a result of the gambler reviewing college basketball rankings during the season, the movement of teams within that ranking system can be tracked. This movement may be used to infer the stability of teams with regard to winning games across all types of competition (See Figure 1, 2024 Team Rankings, page 7). As a case in point, the Matrix shows the erratic play of San Diego St. and Texas Tech, the downward trend of Kansas and Florida Atlantic, the rise of Creighton and Kentucky, and the steady course of UConn, Houston, and Purdue.

Comparing the March Top 25 Ranking Matrix to the actual success of teams in the 2024 Tournament shows that of the teams making it to the fourth round of the Tournament, only North Carolina State was not in a top 25 club at any point in which this review was conducted in this book.

Individual success of the top 25 teams as of March 11, 2024, is indicated by an "ER" followed by a number for the round that the team was actually eliminated from the Tournament (Exit Round). This analysis shows that in the 2024 Tournament, the cream definitely rose to the top, with UConn, ranked #2, and Purdue, ranked #3, facing off in the Championship game. A 2025 Team Ranking Matrix form is provided on page 109 of Appendix B for the gambler to rate teams during the 2025 season.

Turning our attention back to conference tournament championship results, which are the last look at teams before the NCAA Tournament, these games can be misleading as they relate to betting. This is because top teams are not motivated in the same way as teams that know that the only path to make the NCAA Tournament is to win their conference tournament or go deep into its rounds.

Nationally recognized teams that are thought to be locked into a particular position in the Tournament bracket called the "seeding" (See Understanding the Tournament Bracket, page 8) may play with an attitude that they have nothing to prove and without an urgency to win. In preparation for the National Tournament, top teams are much more concerned with being well rested and avoiding injury, particularly to key players, than winning a conference tournament title.

Figure 1

2024 TEAM RANKING MATRIX

Rank	Date 1/29	Date 2/4	Date 2/12	Date 2/19	Date 2/26	Date 3/4	Date 3/11
1	UConn	UConn	UConn	UConn	Houston	Houston	Houston ER 3
2	Purdue	Purdue	Purdue	Houston	Purdue	UConn	UConn ER Champ
3	North Carolina	North Carolina	Houston	Purdue	UConn	Purdue	Purdue ER 6
4	Houston	Kansas	Marquette	Arizona	Tennessee	Tennessee	N. Carolina ER 3
5	Tennessee	Houston	Arizona	Tennessee	Marquette	Arizona	Tennessee ER 3
6	Wisconsin	Tennessee	Kansas	Iowa State	Arizona	Iowa State	Arizona ER 3
7	Duke	Marquette	North Carolina	Marquette	Kansas	N. Carolina	Iowa State ER 3
8	Kansas	Arizona	Tennessee	Duke	Iowa State	Marquette	Creighton ER 3
9	Marquette	Duke	Duke	Kansas	N. Carolina	Duke	Kentucky ER 1
10	Kentucky	Illinois	Iowa State	N. Carolina	Duke	Creighton	Marquette ER 3
11	Arizona	Wisconsin	S. Carolina	Baylor	Auburn	Baylor	Duke ER 4
12	Iowa State	Auburn	Baylor	Illinois	Creighton	Illinois	Auburn ER 1
13	Creighton	Baylor	Auburn	Alabama	Illinois	Auburn	Illinois ER 4
14	Illinois	Iowa State	Illinois	Auburn	Alabama	Kansas	Baylor R 2
15	Texas Tech	S. Carolina	Alabama	Creighton	Baylor	Kentucky	S. Carolina ER 1
16	Auburn	Alabama	Dayton	Dayton	Kentucky	Alabama	Kansas ER 2
17	Utah St.	Kentucky	Creighton	Kentucky	St. Mary's	S. Carolina	Gonzaga ER 3
18	Baylor	Dayton	St. Mary's	St. Mary's	S. Carolina	Wash St.	Utah St. ER 2
19	New Mexico	Creighton	BYU	S. Diego St.	Wash. St.	Gonzaga	Alabama ER 4
20	FL Atlantic	FL Atlantic	{Wisconsin}	S. Carolina	S. Diego St.	BYU	BYU ER 1
21	Dayton	BYU	{Virginia}	Wash. St.	Dayton	{S. Diego St.}	St. Mary's ER 1
22	BYU	{Utah St.}	Kentucky	{CO State.}	Utah St.	Utah St.	Wash St. ER 2
23	{Oklahoma}	{Texas Tech}	{Indiana St.}	{Texas. Tech}	Gonzaga	St. Mary's	Nevada ER 1
24	Alabama	{S. Diego St.}	{FL Atlantic}	Florida	{Florida}	{South Florida}	Dayton ER 2
25	{TCU}	{New Mexico}	{Oklahoma}	{BYU}	{FL Atlantic}	Dayton	Texas Tech ER 1

A team in {brackets} indicates that the squad is out of the top 25 ranking in the subsequent ranking.

To be sure, the teams who care the most about doing well in a conference tournament are those whose NCAA Tournament fortunes depend on it. For some of these teams, success in their conference tournament only affects seeding in the NCAA Tournament. But for many of these teams, their conference tournament is the last chance to dance. In 2024, this was the plight of North Carolina State their mediocre regular season record, only gained entry into the Tournament through their improbable victory in the Atlantic Coast Conference Tournament (See Understanding the Tournament Bracket below). For all conferences, there is an incentive to want one of its middle-tier teams to win its conference tournament championship. This is to get more of their teams in the Big Dance (no offense to the integrity of conference championships).

Once the NCAA Selection Committee picks Tournament teams, the gambler who has not seen games or examined secondary sources of information on college basketball-not done their homework, may still get a good grade with respect to betting. This can be done by identifying attractive betting options by using the strategies of this book to learn how to skillfully interpret the numbers on betting sheets created by the House and odds available through on-line sportsbooks.

UNDERSTANDING THE TOURNAMENT BRACKET

Teams become eligible for the Tournament either by receiving one of 32 automatic bids by virtue of winning a recognized conference tournament championship, or by getting an invitation as one of 36 teams via an "at large" system. An at-large bid to the Tournament is given by the NCAA Committee in their subjective consideration of the abilities of teams over the course of the regular season and possibly as a result of conference tournament play, short of winning the championship.

The NCAA Committee can invite as many at large teams for the 36 bracket spots from a particular conference as it believes is justified, although past results sometimes show it is not. As a case in point, in 2022, the Big 10 Conference had nine invitees to the Dance, but only two programs reached the Tournament's third round.

With automatic bids set and the invitation of at large teams complete, the NCAA Selection Committee ranks or "seeds" the entire field according to their perceived abilities from 1 to 68 (32 + 36). From the initial Tournament seeding, the four lowest-seeded automatic bids and the four lowest at large teams "start" the 2025 Tournament with a preliminary series of contests called the First Four. These games will be played in 2025 on Tuesday, March 18, and Wednesday, March 19, in Dayton, Ohio. The First Four games involve the eight teams that the NCAA Committee considers to be the last contestants worthy of possibly playing in the First Round of the Tournament.

The four lowest-ranked automatic bid teams are matched for two games, and similarly, the four lowest-ranked at large teams are paired for two other contests (See Figure 2, The 2024 NCAA Tournament First Four Bracket, page 9). The victorious automatic bid teams enter the main bracket as #16 seeds. The winners of the at-large contests become the opponents of seeds that vary from Tournament to Tournament which in 2024 pitted the victorious first four at-large teams as seven seeds against tenth seeds in the South and Midwest Regionals.

In 2024, this meant that in the First Round, #16 seed Wagner played #1 seed N. Carolina; #16 seed Grambling St. played #1 seed Purdue; #10 seed Colorado St. played #7 seed Texas); and #10 seed Colorado played #7 seed Florida (See 2024 Bracket 1st Round Detailed Matrix Chart, page 74).

Figure 2

2024 NCAA Tournament First Four Bracket

The team in *italics* was the winner

Mostly, these teams playing in the First Four and their supporters are being given the opportunity to be involved in this incredible spectacle. But the four survivors of these games are not expected to have much of an impact on the proceedings other than being First Round losers when the main Tournament begins on Thursday, March 20, and Friday, March 21, 2025. However, in 2023, Fairleigh Dickenson refused to bow out in the First Round of the Tournament, becoming only the second #16 seed in history to beat a #1 seed with its victory over Purdue. Similarly, in 2023, Pittsburgh dispatched the #6 seed Iowa St. before succumbing in the next game to Xavier.

The finalized Tournament "bracket" results in the seeding of the teams according to a four-region format. The regions are the West, East, South, and Midwest, which, in the First Round of the Tournament, contain 16 seeded teams in each region (See Figure 3, the 2022 NCAA Tournament Bracket Sheet, page 10).

Ultimately, in assembling the main 64-team bracket, the Committee endeavors to separate the teams such that the "better" ones are projected to clash in the later Tournament rounds. Therefore, in each of the four regions, the seeded teams are matched such that in the opening round, #1 seeds play #16 seeds; #2 seeds play #15 seeds; #3 seeds play #14 seeds; #4 seeds play #13 seeds; #5 seeds play #12 seeds; #6 seeds play #11 seeds; #7 seeds play #10 seeds; and #8 seeds play #9 seeds (See Figure 3).

Because there are four regions, there are four teams for each seed number. For example, there are four #1 seeds, with Gonzaga being designated as the best overall #1 seed in 2022. This distinction meant that in the First Round, they were matched up with what the NCAA Selection Committee considered to be the worst team in the entire Tournament remaining from the First Four games in the West region, where it was thought that Gonzaga would have the easiest path to being that region's champion.

9

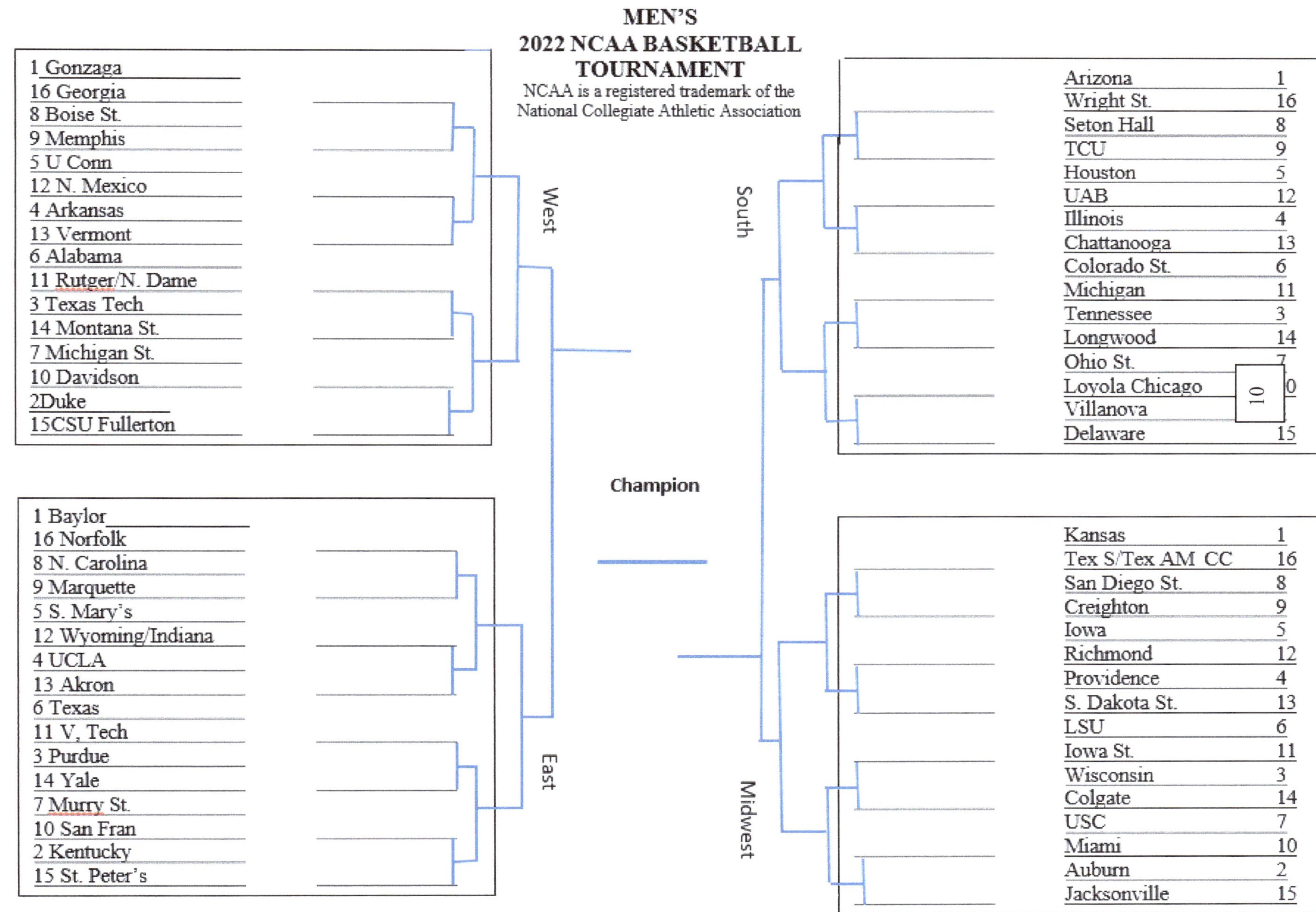

Figure 3

MEN'S
2022 NCAA BASKETBALL
TOURNAMENT
NCAA is a registered trademark of the
National Collegiate Athletic Association

Champion

West

1 Gonzaga
16 Georgia
8 Boise St.
9 Memphis
5 U Conn
12 N. Mexico
4 Arkansas
13 Vermont
6 Alabama
11 Rutger/N. Dame
3 Texas Tech
14 Montana St.
7 Michigan St.
10 Davidson
2 Duke
15 CSU Fullerton

East

1 Baylor
16 Norfolk
8 N. Carolina
9 Marquette
5 S. Mary's
12 Wyoming/Indiana
4 UCLA
13 Akron
6 Texas
11 V, Tech
3 Purdue
14 Yale
7 Murry St.
10 San Fran
2 Kentucky
15 St. Peter's

South

Arizona 1
Wright St. 16
Seton Hall 8
TCU 9
Houston 5
UAB 12
Illinois 4
Chattanooga 13
Colorado St. 6
Michigan 11
Tennessee 3
Longwood 14
Ohio St. 7
Loyola Chicago 0
Villanova 10
Delaware 15

Midwest

Kansas 1
Tex S/Tex AM CC 16
San Diego St. 8
Creighton 9
Iowa 5
Richmond 12
Providence 4
S. Dakota St. 13
LSU 6
Iowa St. 11
Wisconsin 3
Colgate 14
USC 7
Miami 10
Auburn 2
Jacksonville 15

For all teams, "good" Tournament seeding, which for the purposes of this book is a team positioned anywhere from a #1 to a #4 seed. This is the payoff for winning regular season games, especially against worthy opponents, and in some cases, is recognition for a conference championship or success in a conference tournament. Receiving a good seed is desired in the hope of being matched up with a team that can be most easily beaten to advance to the next Tournament round and continue chasing the Championship.

TOURNAMENT ROUNDS

In 2025, after the First Four games are over on Wednesday, there are six rounds of basketball action referred to as the First Round, played on Thursday, March 20, and Friday, March 21; the Second Round, taking place on March 22 and 23; the Third Round, called the Sweet 16 ™, contested Thursday and Friday on March 27 and 28; the Fourth Round called the Elite Eight™ to be settled on March 29 and 30; the Fifth Round called the Final Four™, contested on April 5th; and the Championship Game on April 7th. The ultimate mission of all 64 teams in the Tournament after the First Four is played, is to win six games, becoming the NCAA Basketball Champion.

For the Final Four teams in the Tournament, the way that the bracket is arranged, which varies from year to year, determines which regional winners play in the semi-final games. In 2025, the hypothetical bracket shows the Upper Left Regional Champion playing the Lower Left Regional winner. On the other side of the bracket, the victorious team in the Upper Right Regional is shown as the opponent of the Lower Right Regional Champion (See pages 107 and 108). The final two winners of these contests then settle it all in the Championship game, which in 2025 will be played at the Alamodome in San Antonio, Texas.

The manner in which the Tournament is conducted affects initial wagering. This is because shortly after Selection Sunday, the odds for betting are posted only for the First Four and most of the First Round. But to have access to bet the full 64-team field in the First Round, the gambler must wait until after the First Four games are complete. This meant that in 2024, the West Regional #1 seed North Carolina and the Midwest Regional #7 seed Texas, both starting their Tournament on Thursday, did not know their opponent until the First Four games on Tuesday were over, and it was not until hours later that the House was able to figure out the odds of North Carolina v. Wagner and Texas v. Colorado State games.

Similarly, the Midwest's #1 seed Purdue and the South Regional's #7 seed Florida, both starting their Tournament on Friday, did not know their opponent until the First Four games on Wednesday were over. This allowed odds calculations by the House on the Purdue v. Grambling State and the Florida v. Colorado games.

If you pick up a House bet sheet before the conclusion of the First Four games, the first-round games that are contingent on the outcomes of the First Four games will not be on the bet sheet. The House only cares about games that can be wagered on immediately! This should not be a big issue because, in the First Round, there are plenty of betting options that do not depend on the results of the First Four contests.

BETTING STRATEGIES

FULL-GAME BETTING STRATEGIES

SPREAD BETTING

Setting the spread involves the House determining the number of points given to the dog and subtracted from the favorite to set up a wager opportunity for gamblers. Betting the spread for the complete-game on favorites is the most common form of Tournament betting conducted by a pool of gamblers that includes a huge number of casual bettors. With this influx of novice gamblers, annual Tournament betting has grown to around ten billion dollars.

The lack of gambling sophistication has an influence on the points assigned to games. Therefore, the spread is not actually the number of handicap points to equalize the teams according to their relative abilities. This number is also selected to balance the money bet on each of the teams to make sure that the House is not in danger of having to pay gamblers with its own money in excess of the juice because there is not enough bet on the losing team to pay the winners.

With House financial issues in mind, considerations such as a team's popularity or notoriety can contribute to the House posting a higher opening line point spread on a favorite, e.g., a -7 instead of a -6 or a lower point spread on a dog, e.g., +6 instead of a +7, than a true attempt to equalize the teams based on talent would indicate. This is referred to in this book as "spread bias." The increased risk of a favorite not covering because of spread bias can be addressed by:
- Considering betting on the money line (See below) for the favorite so that the favorite only has to win the contest;
- Betting the spread on the dog. Because they are getting more points than they deserve, or;
- Not betting on the game.

When the dog is receiving fewer points on the spread because of spread bias, the gambler can again decide not to bet on the game, or the bias can be addressed by:
- Betting the spread on the favorite, which is easier to cover when the dog is getting fewer points, or;
- Betting the money line on the favorite will have a higher payout than justified (smaller negative number), and a win by the favorite will be more likely to happen because the assessment of the dog's abilities is giving them too much credit.

In a spread bet on a dog, that team has the two possible positive outcomes of either losing by less than the amount of the spread or actually upsetting the favorite on the court. Spread-betting on either a favorite or a dog has attractive odds, usually around -110. Therefore, a $10 winning spread bet on an individual team pays $9.09, a 90.9% return, although risking the entire investment.

MONEY LINE BETTING

The money line is a relatively obscure betting posture because the average Tournament wager is on a "spread" bet (See above). The money line is analogous to predictions made by a person filling out a Tournament bracket where the goal is only to pick the winners of games. A money line bet is a statement that a team, whether favorite or dog, will "simply" win the game.

Betting the money line on a favorite, contrasts the probability of winning the game against the prospect of being paid a reasonable return. If the House believes that a team will win, the amount of the payout for such an expected victory will be proportionally low according to how certain the House feels about that team prevailing. This is an expression of risk (the money line number) versus reward (the amount paid on a winning ticket). But this is not a strict proportion. This is because an important factor affecting the selection of a particular money line by the House may be the relative popularity of the teams playing, as it influences the amount of money being bet on them. This is referred to in this book as "money line bias."

From a practical sense, complete-game money line odds for favorite teams in some cases, especially in the early rounds, are so high that they make wagering prohibitive, e.g., the money line in the first round for #1 seeds Baylor and Gonzaga in 2022 was -10000. Betting $10,000 to make 100 bucks? Come on! Strategies to address a ridiculous money line on a favorite include:
- Consider betting the spread. This means giving the dog points with more risk of losing;
- Looking for first-half betting options using the favored team (See below) or;
- Not betting on the game, waiting to possibly bet on the favored team in the next round.

With so many betting options in the First Round of the Tournament, there is no pressure to wager on a game when the odds are ridiculous. However, when the money line on a favorite has a reasonable return, e.g., -300, that wager can be exploited to avoid having to defeat a dog by a corresponding point spread of around 7 points (See Table 1 The Relationship Between the Spread and the Money Line for the Favorite and the Dog for the Complete-Game, page 14). But if you consistently have the money line on favorites, you need a sufficient number of wins to offset inevitable losses. Teams with commanding odds, e.g., -600 money lines, do lose!

Betting the money line on the dog is a bold and risky statement that the consensus of the NCAA Committee, the House, and probably that of a vast majority of those betting is wrong. However, when a wildly popular favorite is playing a dog where the teams are more evenly matched than the numbers set by the House would indicate, the opportunity is provided to score big on a dog money line bet. This is because the amount of such a winning bet is multiplied. For example, if a team has a money line of +4000, as St. Peters had in the First Round against Kentucky in 2022, a $10 bet paid $400 when St. Peters pulled off an upset. But don't expect this to happen often!

The safer play for a dog that is undervalued by the House (given a large positive money line when the teams are objectively more evenly matched) is to take the spread points, which will typically be generous if the dog's money line is a high positive number. Therefore, a +400 dog that should be a +340 dog will be given around +9½ points when this should be +8½ points on the spread (See Table 1). By taking the extra point, if the dog wins or does not lose by more than 9 points, the payout will be at -110 odds. This is not nearly the payoff of a +400 dog, but it is far more likely. It should be noted that even when the House makes a money line on a favorite or dog more negative or positive because of its financial considerations, this does not affect the outcome of winning or losing as spread bias does, but it does influence the amount that a gambler is paid.

TABLE 1
THE RELATIONSHIP BETWEEN THE SPREAD AND THE MONEY LINE FOR THE FAVORITE
AND THE DOG FOR THE COMPLETE-GAME

(Continuation of the Chart)

Point Spread	Favorite Money Line	Dog Money Line		Point Spread	Favorite Money line	Dog Money Line
-1	-120/-125	EV/+105		-19½	-4000	+1450/+1500
-1½	-125	+105		-20		
-2	-130/-135	+110/+115		-20½	-4600	+1800
-2½	-130/-145	+120/+125		-21		
-3	-150/-155	+130/+135		-21½	-4800	+2000
-3½	-160/-170	+140/+150		-22		
-4	-180/-185	+160/+180		-22½		
-4½	-200/-245	+175/+205		-23		
-5	-210/-230	+180/+195		-23½		
-5½	-220/-230	+190/+195		-24		
-6	-265/292	+225/+235		-24½	-7800	+2500
-6½	-260/-280	+220/+240		-25		
-7	-300/-330	+250/+270		-25½		
-7½	-320/-350	+260/+290		-26	-13000	+3500
-8	-340/-440	+280/+360		-26½		
-8½	-360/-420	+300/+340		-27		
-9	-420/-440	+360		-27½		
-9½	-440/-550	+360/+425				
-10	-500/-700	+400				
-10½	-500/-600	+450				
-11	-650	+460				
-11½	-650	+475				
-12	-865	+615				
-12½	-900	+625				
-13	-950	+650				
-13½	-1100/-1450	+700/+850				
-14	-1400					
-14½	-1200/-1400	+750/+800				
-15	-1800	+1000				
-15½	-2000	+1050/+1100				
-16	-2000	+1150				
-16½	-1800/-2300					
-17	-1800	+1000				
-17½	-1750/-2500					
-18	-2400	+1150				
-18½	-4000	+1500				
-19						

The forward slash (/) between odds indicates a range of selected numbers by the House.

14

Table 1 demonstrates that when a point spread for a favorite is -1 or -2, the increase in the odds from -110 to -120 or -130 for the corresponding money line bets (an increase in 10 and 20 dollars, respectively, required to maintain a $100 payout) is a reasonable choice as insurance against a push or a loss of the bet on the spread. By choosing the -120 money line instead of a -1 point spread, a push is avoided if the team wins by 1 point. More importantly, by selecting a -130 money line instead of a -2 spread, a loss is prevented when your team only manages a one-point victory.

Table 1 also shows that a spread bet on a favorite with a prohibitively high negative money line is an option to gain attractive odds at -110. This may be reasonable even if this means sweating out spotting a dog a big point spread. For instance, in 2024, all four #1 seeds covered their 20-plus point spreads in the first round (See the First Round Bracket Matrix Charts, pages 73 and 74).

COMPARISON OF HOUSE ADJUSTMENTS TO TEAM BETTING MATCHUPS WITH THE SPREAD AND THE MONEY LINE

House adjustments to betting matchups with the spread are not as precise as the use of money line changes. The spread only moves in one-half point increments while the money line can be adjusted more finely, with payoff changes usually being five dollars per hundred dollars wagered. Moving the spread can also result in huge payoff swings as a one-half point change may be the difference in which team wins the bet, having potentially large implications for gamblers and the House.

The gambler can use the historic numbers in Table 1 and the future numbers that will be on the 2025 House betting sheets to note where a team falls in the money line range for a particular point spread. This is to infer the strength of the selection of the point spread by the House. If a favorite at a -6½ point spread has an associated money line range between -265 and -280 and the House selected money line is -265, requiring $15 less to maintain a $100 payout, this infers that the probability of the team covering -6½ spread is less likely than if the -280 was assigned to the favorite. Logically, the more the House is willing to pay on a favorite (lower negative number, -265 versus -280), the lower the probability of covering. For the gambler, the less you are required to risk to be paid $100, the less likely the House believes the favorite will cover the spread.

For a money line bet on the dog, the lower the payoff range, e.g., +260 versus +290 for a +7½ spread, the more likely the dog is to cover on the spread as the House is paying less for an upset that is more certain. This information could be used to either go with the more likely but lower-paying dog money line or to take the +7½ point spread with more confidence.

The caveat to all this is that the above correlations may also reflect, to an unspecified degree, a response by the House to the dollar amounts expected to be bet on the opening line or reacting to the amount of money actually bet on the money line to balance their finances.

TOTAL BETTING

When betting on the total score "Total" of the game, the issue is whether the combined points of the two teams will be over or under a number determined by the House. Many times, this number ends in half of a point, such as 133½. This is so that the contest, from a gambling perspective, does not end in a push, resulting in no winner and the gamblers just getting their wagers returned. Who wants to go through all that time, effort, and stress of betting on a Total for nothing?

In theory, the over is psychologically the more likely pick for a Total by gamblers and especially novices. This is because as long as the game is in progress, there is usually some hope that the over will be achieved before there are three zeros on the clock. This is in contrast to the finality and pain that can result from having an under where the point Total is exceeded with several minutes to go in a game. 'It can be over before it's over,' but 'It ain't under until it's over!' Furthermore, American sports also accentuate scoring, not preventing or failing to accomplish a "goal." Otherwise, we would be watching more soccer. It is expected that this mentality influences U.S. gamblers to be more inclined toward betting an over in a college basketball game.

Procedurally, if too much money is going on an over, the House will move the Total up to encourage betting the under, e.g., change the over from 133½ to 135. This can signal that it is time to take the under because the Total is now artificially high to balance the wagering. However, the movement of the Total could be the result of other factors, such as player injuries (See page 56).

From the standpoint of probability on a bet for an entire game, Total, there is the specter of overtime, the grim reaper of the under. This factor skews the probability of a Total toward the over. But don't count on Tournament games going into overtime, which is rare.

Regardless of human tendencies, money movement postures by the House, or statistical probabilities, predicting a Total is a very difficult bet. This is because there are so many variables that contribute to this number. Reasons for a Total going over include:
- The favorite and dog are offensively proficient, and the teams are not particularly defensively inclined;
- Early-round mismatches created by the Tournament seeding can result in a favorite "running a dog out of the gym" with a barrage of scoring. This is even more profound when the favorite is not that great defensively, increasing the score by allowing the dog to contribute to the Total;
- If the referees "let them play" by not calling fouls even when they are occurring, the score is expected to be higher, suggesting an over;
- Three-point shots are falling with regularity for one or both of the teams, and;
- A team fouling late in the game to avoid the end of their season can inflate the final score, e.g., if the charity shots are made at a high percentage with no time coming off the clock.

However, the under can occur because of a host of reasons, including:
- Totals based on misplaced reliance on past performance, assuming that statistical results will automatically be replicated in the Tournament. It should be considered that each team in the Dance is facing superior competition compared to their respective statistical averages. Every opponent is one of the special 68 that got into the Tournament. This can manifest itself in poorer-than-average shooting from the field by both teams. Games with unusually high overs, e.g., 155, are suspect to go under;
- The stress of national attention combined with the pressure of single elimination;
- The neutral site arena is likely unfamiliar to either team, affecting shooting;

- Refereeing where "everything is a foul." This disrupts the flow of the game and can get key players in foul trouble, relegating them to the bench or even fouling out of the game. These situations are likely to reduce a team's scoring ability, and;
- There is a contrast in styles of play, with one team being methodical and the opponent being up-tempo. This can lead to a scoring stalemate, generating an under.

To practically analyze the above tendencies, gamblers may employ a hybrid system combining knowledge of the team's statistical trends tempered by the specifics of the particular game matchup as subjectively determined by the gamblers' experience and intuition (luck).

The gambler may also be guided by trends on the House bet sheet. This entails a simplified analysis identifying unusually low or high Totals. For high Totals, the bet may be that the number will not be matched, indicating an under. An unusually low Total may be exceeded because defense may be more difficult against Tournament-worthy teams, suggesting an over. The desperation of single-elimination, e.g., late-in-the-game fouling, may also work against an extremely low Total.

With any strategy, Totals are risky, but the House has little advantage over the gambler. And the silver lining is Totals have a high payout with odds of -110.

FIRST-HALF BETTING STRATEGIES

BETTING THE FIRST-HALF SPREAD

When favored teams are saddled with high complete-game spreads, a first-half spread bet can sometimes make sense. Betting the spread in the first half can reduce the favorite's complete-game spread significantly. For example, a -6½-point complete-game spread may be reduced to -3½-points for a game at intermission, a reduction in the spread by 46% (See Table 2, The Relationship of Complete-Game and First-Half Spreads with the Corresponding First-Half Money Line for the Favorite and the Dog, page 18).

Betting the spread in the first half is also appealing from the standpoint of reducing end-of-game desperation that can change the winner of the bet. But there are still unusual events that do take place at the last seconds of the half that can turn a winning bet into a loss, e.g., a dog sinking a Hail Mary three-point shot at the buzzer.

A first-half spread bet on a dog is reasonable when it appears that the dog is undervalued because they are believed to be receiving more points than is warranted. The strategy is that the favorite will not be able to figure out the dog in the first twenty minutes sufficiently to cover the spread.

Even with the inherent uncertainties of a first-half spread bet on the favorite or dog, the associated -110 odds make the consideration of this type of bet appealing.

TABLE 2
COMPARISON OF COMPLETE-GAME FIRST -HALF SPREADS WITH THE
CORRESPONDING FIRST-HALF MONEY LINES FOR THE FAVORITE AND THE DOG

Game Spread	Half Spread	Half Favorite Money Line	Half Dog Money Line
-½	EV		
-1/ -2½	-½	-115/-125	-105/+105
-2/ -2½	-1	-125/-135	+105/+115
-3	-1½	-135/-145	+115/+122
-3½	-2	-145/-165	+122/+140
-4½/ -5	-2½	-155/-180	+130/+152
-5/ -5½	-3	-180/-195	+152/+162
-6½	-3½	-195/-210	+162/+175
-7/½	-4	-220/-225	+180/+185
-8/ -8½	-4½	-250/-260	+205/+210
-9½	-5	-278/-285	+222/+228
-9½/ -10	-5½	-320	+250
-10/ -11½	-6	-350/-365	+275/+285
-11½	-6½	-385	+300
-12½	-7	-480	+360
-13½/ -14	-7½	-440/-550	+400
-14½	-8	-550	+400
-15	-8½	-480	+360
-15½	-9	-650	+460
-16½	-9½		
-17/ -17½	-10	-900	+600
	-10½		
-20½	-11		
-21½	-11½		
-20½/ -21½	-12	-1100/-1280	+700/+820
	-12½	-1100	+700
-21½	-13		
-23/-24	-13½	-1400/-1450	+800/+850
	-14		
-25½	-14½	-1980	+1090
	-15		
-25/	-15½	-1810	+1005
-21/-27	-16	-1950	+1075
-27½	-16½	-2680	+1280

The forward slash (/) between odds indicates a range of selected numbers by the House.

BETTING THE FIRST-HALF MONEY LINE

In the event of an unreasonably high money line on the favorite for the entire game, a strategy is to bet the first half money line. An unreasonable complete-game money line, e.g., a -6000, may be drastically reduced to around -1100 (81%) by substituting a first-half money line bet (See Table 3). However, as the complete-game money line becomes less negative, the difference in the full game and first-half money line decreases, e.g., a -145 full-game money line may only reduce to -135 (7%) for a wager on the first twenty minutes of a game.

18

TABLE 3

**COMPARISON OF THE COMPLETE-GAME AND
LIKELY CORRESPONDING FIRST-HALF MONEY
LINE ODDS OF THE FAVORITE**

(Continuation of the Chart)

Full Game ML	1st Half ML		Full Game ML	1st Half ML
-120	-115		-500	-300/-320
-125	-120		-540	-315
-130	-125		-600	-335/-350
-135	-130		-650	-325
-140	-120/-125		-700	-330
-145	-135		-735	-410
-150	-140		-800	-360
-155	-140		-865	-345
-160	-145		-900	-400/-480
-165	-140/-150		-1000	-510
-170	-145/-155		-1100	-430
-180	-150/-160		-1200	-550
-190	-160/-165		-1300	-530/-550
-200	-160		-1410	-610
-210	-165/-180		-1500	-550
-215	-180		-2500	-910
-220	-185		-2800	-1280
-230	-185		-6000	-1100
-250	-180/-185		-7000	-800
-260	-185/-195		-7850	-1980
-265	-210		-8000	-1810
-270	-200/-210		-10000	-1950/-2680
-275	-200/-210		-15000	
-280	-190/-200			
-290	-200			
-320	-230			
-330	-220/-230			
-340	-220/-230			
-350	-220			
-360	-240/-245			
-400	-245/-270			
-420	-275			
-425	-280			
-435	-280			
-440	-245/-320			
-450	-335			
-475	-290/-305			

The forward slash (/) between odds indicates a range of selected numbers by the House.

When the first-half money line on a favorite has a reasonable return, e.g., -350, that wager can be exploited to avoid having to defeat a dog by a corresponding point spread of around 6 points (See Table 2, shaded row, page 18). The downside of betting the first-half money line on the favorite is that some teams that are highly favored to actually win a game (teams with large negative complete-game money lines) have a tendency to start slow and thus are accurately given a first-half money line that is considerably less negative than the full game odds. Sometimes, there is a realistic probability that teams that, on paper, have no chance of winning the game may be ahead after the first twenty minutes of play.

In a specific example of a failed first-half money line wager in the Tournament, an analysis of Gonzaga in 2022 demonstrated that in the team's entire season of some thirty games, the Bulldogs were only behind at the half on two occasions. A logical extension of this fact was to bet the money line, asserting that Gonzaga would be ahead in the game by halftime. The result was Gonzaga being behind at the half in this second-round game, making a parlay card a loser, although the team did manage to win the game. In the third-round Gonzaga game, where the first-half money line was bet a second time on a parlay card, the team not only lost again at the half but was eliminated from the Tournament by Arkansas. The best-laid plans of gamblers can still go awry.

A bet on the first-half money line for the dog is an attempt to catch the favorite with their "pants down" in the first twenty minutes. Because being ahead at a game's intermission is more of a coin toss than a demonstration of a particular team's actual superiority, the money line for the dog at intermission pays significantly less than the number for the complete-game.

The difference between the entire game and first-half money line odds for dogs are shown below (See Table 4 Comparison of the Complete-Game and Likely Corresponding First-half Money Line Odds of the Dog, page 21). The Table indicates that first-half dogs are paid less than complete-game dogs as the House feels they are more likely to be ahead at the half. This difference is more significant the greater the odds are against the dog (the larger the positive spread number). The trick is to find a dog that is better than advertised or find a favorite that is notorious for a slow start and/or that plays down to their competition. The return in these situations can be extremely high, but it will likely take some knowledge of the teams and probably some luck to pull this off.

COMPARISON OF SPREAD AND MONEY LINE BETTING FOR THE COMPLETE-GAME AND FIRST HALF

Table 2 differs from Table 1 concerning the complete-game comparison between the spread and the money line for the favorite and the dog. This is because for a given point spread in the first half, the money line for the favorite is more negative (needing a larger bet for a payoff of $100), and the money line for the dog is a larger positive number (indicating a greater payoff for betting $100). The House feels that the favorite is more likely to win at the half for a given spread.

To illustrate the difference in Table 1 and Table 2, a complete-game 4-point spread for the favorite in Table 1 corresponds to around -180, while this 4-point money line is approximately -220 for a first-half bet on the favorite in Table 2. Similarly, a 4-point spread for the dog for the complete-game in Table 1 relates to a money line of around +160. This is in contrast to a money line of around +180 for a dog receiving a +4-point spread for a first-half bet in Table 2.

**COMPARISON OF THE COMPLETE-GAME AND
LIKELY CORRESPONDING FIRST-HALF MONEY
LINE ODDS OF THE DOG**

(Continuation of the Chart)

Full Game ML	1st Half ML		Full Game ML	1st Half ML
+105	EV or +100/-105		+360	
+110	+105		+375	+240/+260
+115	+105		+380	
+120			+400	+250/260
+125	+115		+430	+260
+130	+115		+450	+290
+135	+125/+130		+475	
+140	+125		+500	
+145	+125/+130		+515	+315
+150			+570	+310
+155	+130/+140		+575	+290
+160	+122/+130		+615	+275
+165	+140		+625	+360
+170	+145		+675	+380
+175	+140/+148		+700	+400
+180	+145		+725	+330
+185	+150		+825	+390
+190			+850	+455
+195	+143/+165		+1300	+655/+820
+200	+152		+1800	+1005/+1280
+210	+162/+170		+1948	+1090
+220	+165			
+225	+185			
+230	+175			
+235	+175			
+240	+145/+180			
+245				
+250	+190/+210			
+255	+185			
+260	+185			
+270				
+280				
+290				
+300				
+320	+230			
+340				
+350	+230/+240			

The forward slash (/) between odds indicates a range of selected numbers by the House.

BETTING THE FIRST-HALF TOTAL

Betting the over for the first half involves many of the considerations that are in play for an over bet on the entire game, including:

- The ability of both teams to score but not concentrate on defense;
- The way that the game is officiated, and;
- The matching of a high and low seed.

First-half betting on the over is distinguished from its complete-game counterpart by the fact that there is no possibility of overtime to inflate the score to potentially result in an improbable over. There is also less of a tendency for desperate actions on the part of teams near the end of the half, analogous to fouling to extend the game. All of this contributes to a tendency for fewer points to be scored by halftime. The House recognizes this fact by making the first-half Total approximately 47% of the full game Total. But the unique pressures of the Tournament on the players still make this prediction an inexact science. A strategy to find an over is to look for particularly low complete-game numbers on the House Bet Sheet relative to all of the Total numbers on the sheet, e.g., a complete-game Total of 126, for the possibility of betting that the over will cover the expected 59½-point first-half Total. Here, it really helps to know your teams!

In contrast, a bet on the under hopes the teams will not lose at the beginning of the contest and not get into a comfortable flow of the game. This can mean being out of sorts on offense, translating into nervous and inaccurate shooting and, in particular, poor three-point shooting but defending like there is no tomorrow, which there isn't for the losing team.

A strategy for betting the first half under can involve finding unusually high overs on the House bet sheet, e.g., 155 points for the entire game, and betting the under at the intermission. The expectation is that the first-half Total, which should be around 72½-points, is too high a bar. It is also of note that if the game is an over at the half, the full game is usually likewise an over. This is reflected by the fact that sportsbooks generally do not allow a first-half and full-game bet on Totals for the same game on the same bet ticket. Therefore, if you have a good handle on a Total and you are not allowed to make the aforementioned parlay, you might consider doubling down by making two separate bets, either the over at the half and for the game or bet the under for the half and the entire game (See the 2024 Bracket Matrix Charts, pages 74-78).

Although a bet on a first-half Total, be it an over or under, is somewhat of a crap shoot, the payout at -110 odds is attractive.

BETTING ON INDIVIDUAL GAMES

Bets of all types discussed above can be made on individual games for the entire contest or the first half. This reduces the need to win multiple games on a parlay ticket (see below). Individual first-half bets on the money line are unique in that they allow the gambler to wager on highly favored teams, whereas the same type of bet on the entire game would be impractical. This is because some odds for the complete-game are ridiculously in favor of the House, with payouts that are too small for the risk being taken. First-half bets are also decided after only the first twenty minutes of play, eliminating the anxiety of sitting through the entire game.

If you are betting on a spread, an under, or an over, the wager will generally have favorable odds of -110, nearly doubling your money. However, wagering on spreads or Totals is risky. But even if you are betting on a money line, to reduce the risk on an individual game, the payout is usually only a small percentage of the bet, e.g., a $50 bet on a -500 team only pays $10.

Unless you are prepared to weather the perils of individual bets on spreads and totals or to wager significant dollars on the money line, these bets may not be a very important part of your Tournament betting strategy. This is particularly true in the early rounds when there are so many options for parlay wagering (See below). However, winning on these individual bets at any stage of the Tournament can finance more risky parlay bets. This is playing with House Money.

PARLAY BETTING

The use of the "parlay" bet is one of the best reasons to wager on the Tournament. To move beyond the casual bettor who is simply wagering on the spreads of individual games, you need to venture into the world of parlay bets. To be sure, the tension and excitement of having to win multiple bets on the same bet ticket will likely have you much more engrossed in the Tournament games if not screaming at the television monitors.

Parlay bets can employ money lines, spreads, and Totals for the complete-game and half-time bets. These betting options are available to construct tickets composed of at least two events. Parlaying can significantly multiply the payout of a winning ticket. Of course, a parlay requires that every game on the bet ticket is won. One loss and the party's over!

With respect to the odds of the teams on a parlay card, "similar odds should generally flock together" to increase the chances of winning. This means that a -900 money line team should probably not be paired with a -170 money line team on the same card. In such a combination, the -900 money line team is probably going to win, but the -170 money line team is only slightly favored to win and thus could easily kill the ticket. An example of balanced odds on a three-team money line parlay ticket is -460, -330, and -300. However, a $10 bet on this ticket only has a payout of $11.15.

Violating the concept of paring teams with similar odds can be done intentionally to boost a payout on a bet. For example, a money line four team $50 bet with money line odds of -1100, -1000, -950, and -900 has a payout of $23.68. If a -300 money line team is added to make a five-team parlay, the payoff goes to $48.25. If instead of the -300 money line team, an event with -110 odds is added to the original four-team parlay, the payoff for the new five-team parlay balloons to $90.67. But of course, you have to find the optimal spread or Total event to add to the four-team parlay, which is not easy! A parlay calculator to test the payoff of a potential bet is available at several online betting apps, including www.vegasinsider.com.

In setting up parlay tickets in any round of the Tournament that is played on two days, e.g., games on Thursday and Friday, bets should probably be assembled based on the team matchups, not when the games are played. Not confining bets to teams playing on the same day gives the gambler more options and flexibility. You can wait one day to get paid, and if a Thursday team on a ticket loses, the Friday teams on that ticket can be "reloaded" or bet again on subsequent parlay tickets.

To illustrate the point, Friday teams on such a ticket with a Thursday loss could be combined on a new ticket with other Thursday games not played yet. Another option is for the Friday games on the losing ticket to be bet again with other upcoming Friday games and or Saturday games from Thursday results that have been posted for betting by the House. This could include the team that killed your initial Thursday ticket in the first place.

The progress of game results, for the purpose of reloading, can be tracked by the gambler on the regional Tournament bracket sheets by continuously updating them (See Appendix B, pages 107 and 108). This can be done by checking game results on your phone or consulting the message boards at a sportsbook, usually located behind the bet windows. Monitoring in this way gives maximum flexibility in response to bets that are lost.

With a parlay, bets on the Tournament can be combined with wagers on other events, including those from the NBA, NIT, and NCAA Women's Basketball Tournament (See Sample Bets #18 and #19, page 63). If it looks like a promising bet, maybe it should be added to a Tournament card to increase the potential payout! While NIT games have many teams that may be familiar as squads that barely missed the Tournament, it should be recognized that the incorporation of NCAA women's games and the NBA has betting nuances that are beyond the scope of this book.

PARLAY BETTING, INCLUDING FIRST-HALF BETS AND MULTIPLE BETS ON THE SAME GAME

Incorporating first-half bets in a parlay increases the options available in assembling bets. This is particularly apparent when heavily favored teams are considered that would otherwise have odds for the entire game that are so high that their inclusion would be unreasonable.

It should be noted that many sportsbooks do not allow parlay bets that include multiple outcomes from the same contest, such as the money line and the spread on the same team or a money line bet on the favorite and the spread on the dog. As an example of this type of wager, a two-event parlay bet on Wisconsin with a money line of -330, with the second leg being a bet on the opponent Colgate having a +7 spread. Here, the expectation is that Colgate will lose but by less than 7 points. This has the effect of a two-team parlay at -330 and -110 in the same contest. With a $20 bet on the money line for Wisconsin, the payout is $6.06. But with the addition of the spread on Colgate, the return increases to $29.75. Of course, the card is lost if Colgate wins in an upset or loses by more than 7 points. This strategy can be expanded by adding other games to this two- team parlay to boost the payout even further, assuming the sportsbook takes this type of wager.

MULTIPLE-EVENT -110 ODD PARLAY BETTING

A parlay bet can certainly involve more than three events with varying odds, but a three-event -110 odds parlay is a fair compromise between the risk of losing the ticket and the reasonable probability of a significant payoff. The mission is to find three -110 odds events for a ticket. This requires identifying three wagers involving a spread, over, or under either for the entire game or the first half of a game to put together on a three-team parlay ticket. A $10 bet on a ticket of this nature returns $59.58. With this kind of return, a few losses are acceptable. The payoff numbers for 3 to 8 team parlays with -110 odds are shown below in Table 5, page 25.

TABLE 5
PAYOFFS FOR VARIOUS $10 PARLAYS @ -110 ODDS

3-team parlay	4-team parlay	5-team parlay	6-team parlay	7-team parlay	8-team parlay
-110	-110	-110	-110	-110	-110
-110	-110	-110	-110	-110	-110
-110	-110	-110	-110	-110	-110
	-110	-110	-110	-110	-110
		-110	-110	-110	-110
			-110	-110	-110
				-110	-110
					-110
Payoff $59.58	Payoff $122.83	Payoff $243.59	Payoff $474.13	Payoff $914.24	Payoff $1754.46

HEDGING BETS

Games can be "hedged," where the money line is a bet on the favorite on one parlay ticket, with the dog in that game bet on the spread on another parlay ticket with other games. You are **not** betting against yourself, as the favorite can win, and if they do not cover, you win the hedge part of both bets. Hedging is most plausible when there is a significant spread, e.g., 7 points. To illustrate the strategy, in the Second Round of the 2024 Tournament, -265 Tennessee could be paired with -9 Arizona and -4½ Baylor. A hedge in the Tennessee game would be another bet ticket with opponent +6½ Colorado on a two-leg parlay with -450 Houston. The result of this bet was Tennessee won on the money line, and Colorado, as a dog, covered the spread because they only lost by 4 points. Because all the legs on both parlays won, both tickets were winners!

Hedging bets is some protection against favorites winning their game but not covering on a spread bet. However, if the dog actually wins, the bet containing the money line on the favorite is, of course, lost, and if the dog loses by more than the spread, only the ticket with the favorite has the potential to win. In a hedge scenario, even if the favorite wins and the dog covers, you still have to win the other legs on the separate parlay cards to cash the tickets.

To improve the probability of a win on at least one of the cards when hedging is being used, the parlay with the money line on the favorite in the hedge can be restricted to three legs, with the parlay giving the points to the dog only being paired with one additional game, usually on a fairly heavily favored outcome, e.g., -450 Houston, for a two-leg parlay as in the hedge example above.

A hedge bet can also be made with an individual bet, usually on a favorite team. Here, a straight bet is made on the spread with a second separate straight bet on the money line of the same team. The hope is that the team will win both bets, but if the team does not cover, they will win the money line. Of course, if you have faith in an individual dog, a hedge on that team may be a desirable wager. This, again, entails a spread and a corresponding bet on the money line. The hope is that the dog will win to generate a handsome payoff with significant plus money or at least cover the spread at -110 odds. It should be recognized that if the dog does not even cover, both of the hedged tickets in this scenario are lost.

ODDS INVERSION

Odds inversion happens when the lower-seeded team is the dog on the spread in a game. For example, in the First Round of the 2024 Tournament, #6 seed Clemson was +2 on the spread in its matchup with #11 seed New Mexico. The fact that this type of situation is unusual is a testament to the care and accuracy of the NCAA Committee's seeding procedures. Moreover, this is done without the benefit of knowing the matchups that will actually materialize in the Tournament that the sportsbook oddsmakers are privy to when they make their determinations.

Odds inversion was in play eight times during the 2024 Tournament, with the NCAA and the sportsbooks both correctly predicting the outcomes of the games four times. With the same analysis for odds inversion in the 2023 Tournament, the House established the lower seed as the dog eight times while being correct in six of those games for a 75% winning percentage. However, without specific analysis, these games are more of a curiosity than a statistically relevant trend.

THE DISPLAY OF BETTING INFORMATION IN THIS BOOK

This book exposes the gambling opportunities the Tournament provides by displaying information on the games in a unique and highly organized matrix format of columns and rows that form cells. This is called a Bracket Matrix Chart. Possibilities of winning bets are much harder to realize if they are camouflaged by the maze of haphazard data that characterizes many existing presentations of gambling options on House betting sheets.

The position of each cell of a matrix chart is identified by two numbers: the first is the column from left to right, and the second number is the row from top to bottom. For example, a designation on the 2024 First Round Matrix Chart of 3, 3 would be the game between #3 seed Kentucky and #14 seed Oakland. Similarly, a 3, 1 cell for the Fourth Round in 2024 would be the game between #4 seed Duke and #11 seed North Carolina State. Each cell of a matrix chart condenses a large amount of gambling information by showing the money line, spread, and Total established by the House for the entire game and the first half, all in one place.

In the First Round of the Tournament, the rows of the matrix display the seeding of the teams across each region, starting with the four #1 seeds with their #16 seed opponents in the first row and finishing with the four #8 seeds facing the #9 seeds in the eighth row. Each of the four columns in the First Round shows a group of teams trying to reach the Final Four (See the 2024 1st Round Bracket Detailed Matrix Chart, page 74).

The matrix charts each continue to display the teams' original seeding as the Tournament progresses. For example, in 2024, when #3 seed Kentucky lost to #14 seed Oakland in the First Round, the matrix chart in the Second Round shows #14 seed Oakland at the top of cell 3, 3 playing #11 North Carolina State, the victors in their first-round upset win over #6 seed Texas Tech at the bottom of the cell (See the 2024 NCAA Tournament 2nd Round Bracket Matrix Chart, page 75).

The number of rows of a matrix chart decreases from eight in the First Round to four in Round Two, to two in Round Three, and finally to one for Rounds Four through Six. The columns of the matrix decrease from four for the first four rounds to two in the Fifth Round and only one column for the Championship game.

For the fifth and sixth Rounds, the columns no longer represent the Tournament regions because the regional winners of the Final Four games vary. It takes five pages to display all of the Tournament rounds in the matrix configuration (See Appendix A, pages 73-78).

BETTING MONEY LINE, SPREADS, AND TOTALS IN GENERAL CONSIDERATION OF TOURNAMENT ROUNDS

Betting strictly according to initial Tournament seeding can be refined by taking the House odds on the contest into consideration. The money line is the same as simply betting on which team will win. But making money is not that simple as prohibitive favorites pay very little, and the dogs with large negative money line numbers seldom win. The spread has more attractive -110 odds, but unless you are lucky, spread betting requires some knowledge about how to interpret House odds and use betting strategies, which change to some degree during the Tournament rounds.

In customizing a betting strategy, the gambler may also consider the statistics that are graphically displayed in Table 6, pages 35-40. However, these numbers should be used with caution! Any value in the numbers generated here as predictive of future betting trends is based on the continuing accuracy of the NCAA Committee seeding process combined with the anticipation of future correct assessments of the probabilities of gaming odds by industry-recognized odds makers.

The determination of gambling "trends" is also influenced by the number of trials that are the basis of a given probability, e.g., in the Fourth Round, there are only four games to establish the money line winning percentage as opposed to the thirty-two games for review in the First Round. Further, in the analysis of any individual row of a Tournament round, there are a maximum of four games to consider. Making decisions based on small sampling sizes loses predictive power because of what is called "sampling error."

Even with all of the drawbacks of depending on past Tournament numbers, their careful consideration can still improve 2025 betting decisions.

BETTING DURING THE FIRST ROUND

The First Round of the Tournament is the best opportunity for the gambler to win money, with the NCAA Selection Committee and the House essentially making your gambling selections for you! This is because the Committee has purposely set up mismatches resulting from the manner in which the Tournament bracket is arranged. Mismatches result from seeding that pits the best teams against what is expected to be inferior competition. These matchups are supposed to become more and more even, moving down from the top of the matrix from the #1 seed to the #8 seed. The most evenly matched games, in theory, are the #8 seeds playing the #9 seeds.

Additionally, gambling opportunities materialize because the House typically establishes odds with the largest money lines and spreads of any round that can be used to further inform betting decisions. The gambler's odds of winning in this round are increased even more by the sheer number of games, allowing the gambler to exploit personal knowledge about contests to their advantage. The thirty-two contests at this stage are the most of any Tournament round.

Collectively, for the thirty-two games of the First Round for 2024, 2023, and 2022, respectively, winning **complete-game money line** percentages for favorites were: 65.6%, 78.1%, and 71.9%. Winning **spread** percentages for favorites in 2024, 2023, and 2022, respectively, were: 59.4%, 56.25%, and 50%. And the times when **Totals** were overs for 2024, 2023, and 2022 were: 62.5%, 28.1%, and 50%, respectively.

In examining the **first half** of first-round games in 2024, 2023, and 2022, respectively, winning **money line** percentages for favorites were: 75%, 68.75%, and 65.6%. Favorite winning **spread** percentages in 2024, 2023, and 2022, respectively, were: 46.8%, 43.75 %, and 37.5%. And the times when **Totals** were overs for 2024, 2023, and 2022 were: 68.8%, 40.6%, and 37.5%.

Within this First Round, there are also more specific trends that develop when examining the outcomes of the games according to individual seeds, as explored below.

BETTING ON THE #1 SEEDS IN THE FIRST ROUND

For the #1 seeds in the First Round, the money line for the entire game in 2022, 2023, and 2024 is typically an unreasonable bet, frequently around -10000. Even a first-half money line is not attractive at around -2000. Moreover, the #1 seeds typically must spot the #16 seeds over 20 points for the complete game. This is a bar which for 2022 and 2023 was achieved around 50% of the time. Although, in 2024, all four of the #1 seeds covered. For the first half, a strategy to try to catch the #1 seeds off-guard by betting the spread on the #16 seeds has about a 50% success rate. Complete games and games at the half involving #1 seeds also typically exceed the Total around 50% of the time. Except in 2022, all four of the first-half contests resulted in unders.

Because of the unremarkable trends of #1 seeds in the First Round, probably the best thing to do at this point is to not bet on these contests without specific knowledge about games and wait to see if there are attractive gambling opportunities with these #1 seeded teams in the Second Round. This means considering closely watching the #8 seed versus #9 seed games that will produce the second-round opponents of the #1 seeds (See Table 6, pages 35-40).

BETTING ON THE #2 SEEDS IN THE FIRST ROUND

For the #2 seeds in 2024, 2023, and 2022, respectively, **complete-game** winning **money line** percentages in the first round were: 100%, 75%, and 75%. The #2 seed **spread** winning percentages in 2024, 2023, and 2022, respectively, were: 75%, 75%, and 50%. And **overs** for 2024, 2023, and 2022 were: 50%, 25%, and 50%, respectively.

In examining the **first half** of first-round games, the #2 seeds in 2024, 2023, and 2022, winning **money line** percentages were: 100%, 75%, and 75%. Winning **spread** percentages for #2 seeds in 2024, 2023, and 2022, respectively, were: 50%, 75%, and 66%. And the times when **Totals** were overs for 2024, 2023, and 2022 were: 75%, 75%, and 50%, respectively.

Bets on the money line of #2 seeds are very likely to win. However, because these wagers have high odds, around -2500, the payout is unattractively small. Alternatively, the money line for the first half can be selected, bringing the odds down to -1000 with no reduction in the winning percentage in this analysis (See the highlighted numbers). These payouts can be greatly improved by betting the complete-game spread, bringing the odds all the way down to -110 without too much of a reduction in the probability of winning. The bottom line is that individual bets and parlays of #2 seed teams, utilizing money lines and the complete-game spread, are very likely to prevail.

BETTING ON THE #3 SEEDS IN THE FIRST ROUND

For the #3 seeds in 2024, 2023, and 2022, respectively, **complete-game** winning **money line** percentages were: 75%, 100%, and 100%. The #3 seed **spread** winning percentages in 2024, 2023, and 2022, respectively, were: 75%, 75%, and 100%. And the times when **Totals** for #3 seeds resulted in overs for 2024, 2023, and 2022 were: 50%, 25%, and 50%, respectively.

In the **first half** of first-round games, the #3 seeds in 2024, 2023, and 2022, respectively, winning **money line** percentages were: 75%, 100%, and 100%. Winning **spread** percentages for #3 seeds in 2024, 2023, and 2022, respectively, were: 47.75%, 45.75 %, and 42.75%. And the times when **Totals** were overs for 2024, 2023, and 2022 were: 75%, 75%, and 75%.

Money line odds on #3 seeds for the complete-game are often high at around -800, resulting in small payouts but with a very high probability of winning. In fact, for the complete-game, the #3 seed did not lose a single game in 2022 or 2023! However, in 2024, this complete-game record was blemished by the loss of Kentucky to Oakland, although the other three #3 seeds did win their games. For the complete-game, the spread bet reduces the odds to -110 with very little reduction in the probability of winning, arguably making this type of wager a more attractive option.

The money line for the #3 seeds at the half is under -400, with a significant but manageable reduction in winning percentage statistically, making this another attractive wagering option.

BETTING ON THE #4 SEEDS IN THE FIRST ROUND

For the #4 seeds in 2024, 2023, and 2022, respectively, **complete-game** winning **money line** percentages were: 75%, 75%, and 100%. The #4 seed **spread** winning percentages in 2024, 2023, and 2022, respectively, were: 50%, 75%, and 25%. And the times when **Totals** for #4 seeds resulted in overs for 2024, 2023, and 2022 were: 75%, 50%, and 25%, respectively.

In the **first half** of first-round games, the #4 seeds in 2024, 2023, and 2022, winning **money line** percentages were: 100%, 75%, and 25%. Winning **spread** percentages for #2 seeds in 2024, 2023, and 2022, respectively, were: 50%, 75%, and 25%. And the times when **Totals** were overs for 2024, 2023, and 2022 respectively, were: 100%, 25%, and 25%.

Complete-game money lines for the #4 seeds usually win with odds ranging from -300 to -900 with mediocre payouts (See the highlighted numbers). Betting on the first half money line improves the odds, ranging from -220 to around -400, with a small reduction in the winning percentage. The complete-game and half-time spread bets are basically a 50/50 proposition.

BETTING ON THE #5 SEEDS IN THE FIRST ROUND

For the #5 seeds in 2024, 2023, and 2022, respectively, **complete-game money line** winning percentages were: 75%, 100%, and 50%. The #5 seed **spread** winning percentages in 2024, 2023, and 2022, respectively, were: 50%, 75%, and 50%. And the times when **Totals** for #5 seeds resulted in overs for 2024, 2023, and 2022 were: 75%, 0%, and 75%, respectively.

In the **first half** of first-round games, the #5 seeds in 2024, 2023, and 2022, winning **money line** percentages were: 75%, 75%, and 75%. The #5 seed winning **spread** percentages in 2024, 2023, and 2022, respectively, were: 50%, 25%, and 0%. And the times when **Totals** were overs for 2024, 2023, and 2022 were: 25%, 0%, and 0%, respectively.

While the #5 seeds are in the grey caution area of the matrix, as well as traditionally being thought to be vulnerable to losses to #12 seeds, this is not strongly supported by complete-game money line statistics from the past three years. Analysis of contests between #5 seeds and #12 seeds is potentially of more interest in putting together brackets rather than bets. In contrast to the perceived weakness of #5 seeds, they have been dominant with respect to the first-half money line. However, #12 seeds have been very successful in covering the first half spread. The propensity for Totals that are unders in the first half is also a notable trend in this analysis of #5 seeds (See highlighted numbers).

BETTING ON THE #6 SEEDS IN THE FIRST ROUND

For the #6 seeds in 2024, 2023, and 2022, respectively, **complete-game** favorite winning **money line** percentages were: 25%, 75%, and 50%. The #6 seed **spread** winning percentages in 2024, 2023, and 2022, respectively, were: 50%, 50%, and 50%. And the times when **Totals** for #6 seeds resulted in overs for 2024, 2023, and 2022 were: 75%, 0%, and 25%, respectively.

In the **first half** of first-round games, the #6 seeds in 2024, 2023, and 2022, respectively, winning **money line** percentages were: 75%, 50%, and 25%. Winning **spread** percentages for favorites in 2024, 2023, and 2022, respectively, were: 50%, 25%, and 25%. And the times when **Totals** were overs for 2024, 2023, and 2022 were: 75%, 50%, and 50%, respectively.

The betting outcomes for the #6 seeds mimic a 50/50-coin toss.

BETTING ON THE #7 SEEDS IN THE FIRST ROUND

For the #7 seeds in 2024, 2023, and 2022, respectively, **complete-game** winning **money line** percentages were: 75%, 75%, and 75%. The #7 seed **spread** winning percentages in 2024, 2023, and 2022, respectively, were: 50%, 50%, and 75%. And the times when **Totals** for #7 seeds resulted in overs for 2024, 2023, and 2022 were: 50%, 50%, and 50%, respectively.

In the **first half** of first-round games, the #7 seeds in 2024, 2023, and 2022, winning **money line** percentages were: 100%, 25%, and 25%, respectively. Winning **spread** percentages for #7 seeds in 2024, 2023, and 2022, respectively, were: 100%, 25%, and 0%. And the times when **Totals** were overs for 2024, 2023, and 2022 were: 50%, 50%, and 25%, respectively.

Once again, there is no compelling trend for betting #7 seeds, with the only semblance of a trend being the complete-game money line.

BETTING ON THE #8 SEEDS IN THE FIRST ROUND

For the #8 seeds in 2024, 2023, and 2022, respectively, **complete-game** favorite winning **money line** percentages were: 25%, 50%, and 50%. The #8 seed **spread** winning percentages in 2024, 2023, and 2022, respectively, were: 50%, 50%, and 50%. And the times when **Totals** for #8 seeds resulted in overs for 2024, 2023, and 2022 were: 75%, 25%, and 50%, respectively.

In the **first half** of first-round games, the #8 seeds in 2024, 2023, and 2022, respectively, winning **money line** percentages were: 0%, 75%, and 75%. Winning **spread** percentages for #8 seeds in 2024, 2023, and 2022, respectively, were: 0%, 75%, and 75%. And the times when **Totals** were overs for 2024, 2023, and 2022 were: 75%, 0%, and 50%, respectively.

The money line winning percentages for the game and at halftime for the #8 seeds support the notion that these seeds habitually have difficulty with the #9 seeds, making these bets a 50/50 proposition. Similarly, percentages on the spreads and Totals for both the complete-game and at the half indicate that these bets are also pretty much a toss-up (See Table 6, pages 39-40.

FINAL BETTING ISSUES DURING THE FIRST ROUND

It is suggested that the entire two-day field should be considered when assembling bet tickets during the First Round without regard to whether a game is played on Thursday or Friday for maximum flexibility. When the Thursday contests win on a bet ticket that also has Friday contests, such a parlay can be well on the way to prevailing on a parlay spanning both days of the round. If there are any Thursday events that lose on a bet ticket that also contains Friday contests, the gambler has the option of making another bet ticket (reloading See pages 23 and 24 again wagering on the upcoming Friday contests.

The opportunity is here for the gambler to simply make chalk bets (See page 3 involving #1-4 seeds for complete-games and for the first half on individual and parlay bets. This includes wagers with 5, 6, 7, and even 8 legs with a reasonable likelihood of succeeding (See Sample 2024 NCAA College Basketball Bets, Example #2, Page 59. Although the likelihood of winning contests in this First Round is high, the gambler is advised to test the payoff of individual and parlay bets with an online parlay calculator to determine that the bet makes economic sense before placing it.

BETTING DURING THE SECOND ROUND

For the sixteen games of the Second Round for 2024, 2023, and 2022, respectively, **complete-game** winning **money line** percentages for favorites were: 87.5%, 62.5%, and 68.8%. Winning **spread** percentages for favorites in 2024, 2023, and 2022, respectively, were: 58.75%, 31.3%, and 37.5%. The times when **Totals** were overs for 2024, 2023, and 2022 were: 56.25%, 37.5%, and 56.25%, respectively.

In examining the **first half** of the second-round games in 2024, 2023, and 2022, respectively, winning **money line** percentages for favorites were: 81.25%, 50%, and 68.75%. Winning **spread** percentages for favorites in 2024, 2023, and 2022, respectively, were: 37.5%, 37.5%, and 50%. And the times when **Totals** were overs for 2024, 2023, and 2022 were: 34.38%, 31.25%, and 56.25%, respectively.

In contrast to the first round, in the second round of the Tournament for the past three years, dogs were much more of a factor in winning both money line and spread bets for the complete-game and at the Half. This is likely because of the increased parity of the matchups, e.g., possible games between #4 and #5 seeds. To improve the probability of profiting from bets at this stage, more specific trends develop when examining the outcomes of the games according to individual rows of the bracket matrix, as explored below.

BETTING ON FAVORITES IN ROW #1 OF THE SECOND ROUND

For Row #1 favorite teams in 2024, 2023, and 2022, respectively, **complete-game** winning **money line** percentages were: 100%, 75%, and 75%. The Row #1 favorite teams' **spread** winning percentages in 2024, 2023, and 2022, respectively, were: 75%, 50%, and 0%. And the times when **Totals** for the Row #1 matchups resulted in overs for 2024, 2023, and 2022 were: 75%, 25%, and 100%, respectively.

In the **first half** of second-round games for Row #1 favorite teams in 2024, 2023, and 2022, winning **money line** percentages were: 100%, 75%, and 50%, respectively. The Row #1 favorite teams' **spread** winning percentages in 2024, 2023, and 2022, respectively, were: 75%, 50%, and 0%. And the times when **Totals** for Row #1 matchups in this second round were overs for 2024, 2023, and 2022, respectively, were: 75%, 25%, and 75%.

The complete-game money line for the favorite has odds around -500 with an extremely high winning percentage (See the highlighted numbers above). The first half money line, with odds around -320, also trends toward a high winning percentage. Fuel for this trend is provided by the fact that on this row, #1 seeds are playing either #8 or #9 seeds. Additionally, the complete-game and first-half Totals exhibit signs of a trend toward the over. Additional analysis of Row #1 trends to exploit with bets reveals little.

BETTING ON FAVORITES IN ROW #2 OF THE SECOND ROUND

For the Row #2 favorite teams in 2024, 2023, and 2022 respectively, **complete-game** winning **money line** percentages were: 100%, 50%, and 50%. The Row #2 favorite teams' **spread** winning percentages in 2024, 2023, and 2022 respectively, were: 50%, 0%, and 50%. And the times when **Totals** for the Row #2 matchups resulted in overs for 2024, 2023, and 2022 were: 25%, 25%, and 50%, respectively.

In the **first half** of second-round games, Row #2 favorite teams in 2024, 2023, and 2022, winning **money line** percentages, respectively, were: 100%, 50%, and 50%. The Row #2 favorite teams' **spread** winning percentages in 2024, 2023, and 2022, respectively, were: 100%, 50%, and 50%. And the times when **Totals** for Row #2 matchups in this second round were overs for 2024, 2023, and 2022 were: 75%, 25%, and 50%, respectively.

In this second row, obvious trends for the three years being investigated do not emerge even with the likely matchups of #2 seeds with #7 or #10 seeds, except that the money line for the complete-game and at the Half does not show a single loss in 2024 (See the highlighted number above). Another semblance of a trend is the high probability of the complete-game Total being an under.

BETTING ON FAVORITES IN ROW #3 OF THE SECOND ROUND

For Row #3 favorite teams in 2024, 2023, and 2022, respectively, **complete-game** winning **money line** percentages for the favorites were: 50%, 75%, and 50%. The Row #3 favorite teams' **spread** winning percentages in 2024, 2023, and 2022, respectively, were: 50%, 25%, and 25%. And the times when **Totals** for the Row #3 matchups resulted in overs for 2024, 2023, and 2022 were: 75%, 75%, and 50%, respectively.

In the first half of second-round games for Row #3 favorite teams in 2024, 2023, and 2022, winning **money line** percentages were: 50%, 25%, and 75%, respectively. The Row #3 favorite teams' **spread** winning percentages in 2024, 2023, and 2022, respectively, were: 50%, 25%, and 50%. And the times when **Totals** for Row #3 matchups in this Second Round were overs for 2024, 2023, and 2022 were: 50%, 25%, and 50%, respectively. In the Row #3 games, there is no clear trend.

BETTING ON FAVORITES IN ROW #4 OF THE SECOND ROUND

For Row #4 favorite teams in 2024, 2023, and 2022, respectively, **complete-game** winning money line percentages were: 100%, 50%, and 100%. The Row #4 favorite teams' **spread** winning percentages in 2024, 2023, and 2022, respectively, were: 100%, 50%, and 75%. And the times when **Totals** for the Row #4 matchups resulted in overs for 2024, 2023, and 2022 were: 50%, 25%, and 25%, respectively.

In the **first half** of second-round games for Row #4 favorite teams in 2024, 2023, and 2022, winning **money line** percentages were: 75%, 50%, and 100%, respectively. The Row #4 favorite teams' **spread** winning percentages in 2024, 2023, and 2022, respectively, were: 75%, 25%, and 100%. And the times when **Totals** for Row #4 matchups in this second round were overs for 2024, 2023, and 2022 were: 75%, 50%, and 50%, respectively.

The complete-game money line for the favorite had odds around -250, and the complete-game money line has a strong trend, winning all but two games in the last three years (See the highlighted numbers). For the other statistical measurements, results are, for the most part, a 50/50 proposition.

BETTING DURING THE THIRD ROUND

Collectively, in the Third Round of 2024, 2023, and 2022, respectively, **complete-game** winning **money line** percentages for favorites were: 37.5%, 50%, and 37.5%. Winning **spread** percentages for favorites in 2024, 2023, and 2022, respectively, were: 37.5%, 37.5%, and 25%. The times when **Totals** were overs for 2024, 2023, and 2022 were: 25%, 75%, and 12.5%, respectively.

In examining the **first half** of the third-round games in 2024, 2023, and 2022, respectively, winning **money line** percentages for favorites were: 37.5%, 50%, and 75%. Winning **spread** percentages for favorites in 2024, 2023, and 2022, respectively, were: 37.5%, 37.5%, and 50%. And the times when **Totals** were overs for 2024, 2023, and 2022 were: 37.5%, 62.5%, and 0%, respectively.

By the Third Round for both the complete-game and at intermission, the dogs have the slight edge in winning the money line and spread bets, with Totals trending toward the under.

BETTING ON FAVORITES IN ROW #1 OF THE THIRD ROUND

For Row #1 favorite teams in 2024, 2023, and 2022, respectively, **complete-game** winning **money line** percentages were: 50%, 50%, and 25%. The Row #1 favorite teams' **spread** winning percentages in 2024, 2023, and 2022, respectively, were: 50%, 25%, and 0%. **Totals** for the Row #1 matchups resulting in overs for 2024, 2023, and 2022 were: 25%, 50%, and 0%, respectively.

In the **first half** of third-round games for Row #1 favorite teams in 2024, 2023, and 2022, winning **money line** percentages were: 75%, 50%, and 50%, respectively. The Row #1 favorite teams' **spread** winning percentages in 2024, 2023, and 2022, respectively, were: 75%, 50%, and 50%. And the times when **Totals** for Row #1 matchups in this second round were overs for 2024, 2023, and 2022 were: 75%, 50%, and 0%, respectively.

There are no clear trends for the games and the scores in this portion of the Third-Round matrix.

BETTING ON FAVORITES IN ROW #2 OF THE THIRD ROUND

For Row #2 favorite teams in 2024, 2023, and 2022, respectively, **complete-game** winning **money line** percentages were: 25%, 50%, and 50%. The Row #2 favorite teams' **spread** winning percentages in 2024, 2023, and 2022, respectively, were: 25%, 50%, and 50%. And the times when **Totals** for the Row #2 matchups resulted in overs for 2024, 2023, and 2022 were: 25%, 100%, and 25%, respectively.

In the **first half** of third-round games for Row #2, favorite teams in 2024, 2023, and 2022, winning **money line** percentages were: 0%, 50%, and 100%, respectively. The Row #2 favorite teams' **spread** winning percentages in 2024, 2023, and 2022, respectively, were: 0%, 50%, and 75%. And the times when **Totals** for Row #2 matchups in this Third Round were overs for 2024, 2023, and 2022 were: 0%, 75%, and 0%, respectively.

No clear trend is evident for this stage of the Tournament.

BETTING DURING THE 4TH, 5TH, AND 6TH ROUNDS

In the last three rounds of the Tournament, attempting to identify gambling trends with a matrix is very difficult. This is because matchups generally become more even and there are fewer games to try to establish a pattern. For these later rounds, success is dependent on analyzing the team's prior Tournament victories, exploiting opportunities presented by the House in setting odds, and just being lucky.

TABLE 6
GAME BETTING STATISTICS BY ROUNDS

2024 COMPLETE-GAME BETTING STATISTICS BY ROUNDS

Round/Seed/Row	**Specific Rounds** Favorite **Money Line** Winning Percentage	**Seed or Row** Favorite **Money Line** Winning Percentage	**Specific Rounds** Favorite **Spread** Winning Percentage	**Seed or Row** Favorite **Spread** Covering Percentage	**Specific Rounds** Total Overs	**Seed or Row** Over Winning Percentage
1st Round Cells	**65.6%**		**59.38%**		**62.5%**	
#1 Seeds		*100%		100%		75%
#2 Seeds		*100%		75%		50%
#3 Seeds		75%		75%		50%
#4 Seeds		75%		50%		75%
#5 Seeds		75%		50%		75%
#6 Seeds		25%		50%		75%
#7 Seeds		75%		50%		50%
#8 Seeds		25%		25%		75%
2nd Round Cells	**87.5%**		**56.25%**		**56.25%**	
Row #1		100%		75%		75%
Row #2		100%		50%		25%
Row #3		50%		50%		75%
Row #4		100%		100%		50%
3rd Round Cells	**37.5%**		**37.5%**		**25%**	
Row #1		50%		50%		25%
Row #2		25%		25%		25%
4th Round Cells	**75%**		**75%**		**25%**	
Row #1		75%		75%		25%
5th Round Cells	**100%**		**100%**		**0%**	
Row #1		100%		100%		0%
6th Round Cells	**100%**		**100%**		**0%**	
Row #1		100%		100%		0%

Caution: The statistics in this table are only general data points for consideration but are not intended as a substitute for the specific analysis of individual betting options.

In this table, the percentages for money lines are objective because regardless of the actual odds numbers of a specific wager, a team either won, lost, or the result was a push. However, winning percentages on spreads and Totals for favorites may vary. This is because they are dependent on the actual odds numbers received from the House on a particular bet.

35

Round/Seed/Row	**Specific Rounds** Favorite **Money Line** Winning Percentage	**Seed or Row** Favorite **Money Line** Winning Percentage	**Specific Rounds** Favorite **Spread** Winning Percentage	**Seed or Row** Favorite **Spread** Covering Percentage	**Specific Rounds** Total Overs	**Seed or Row** Over Winning Percentage
1st Round Cells	75%		54.8%		70.9%	
#1 Seed		*100%		50%		75%
#2 Seed		*75%		50%		75%
#3 Seed		75%		25%		75%
#4 Seed		100%		50%		100%
#5 Seed		75%		50%		25%
#6 Seed		50%		50%		75%
#7 Seed		100%		100%		50%
#8 Seed		0%		0%		75%
2nd Round Cells	81.25%		37.5%		34.38%	
Row #1		100%		75%		75%
Row #2		100%		100%		75%
Row #3		50%		50%		50%
Row #4		75%		75%		75%
3rd Round Cells	37.5%		37.5%		75%	
Row #1		75%		75%		75%
Row #2		0%		0%		0%
4th Round Cells	100%		75%		25%	
Row #1		100%		75%		25%
5th Round Cells	100%		50%		50%	
Row #1		100%		50%		50%
6th Round Cells	100%		100%		0%	
Row #1		100%		100%		0%

Green highlighted numbers show potentially strong positive trends for the money line and spread of favorite teams.
Red highlighted numbers indicate a potentially strong trend for a money line or spread for dogs.
Yellow highlighted numbers mark potential trends for betting on the Total going under.
Blue highlighted numbers mark potential trends for betting on the Total going over.
*Indicates cells not highlighted because the odds are so unfavorable that the probability does not present a strong trend for wagering, e.g., a 75% probability for -10000 odds having a very small payoff.

Rows after the Third Round are not highlighted in recognition of sampling error.

2023 COMPLETE-GAME BETTING STATISTICS BY ROUNDS

Round/Seed/Row	**Specific Rounds** Favorite **Money Line** Winning Percentage	**Seed or Row** Favorite **Money Line** Winning Percentage	**Specific Rounds** Favorite **Spread** Winning Percentage	**Seed or Row** Favorite **Spread** Covering Percentage	**Specific Rounds** Complete-game Total Overs	**Seed or Row Over** Winning Percentage
1st Round Cells	**78.1%**		**56.25%**		**28.1%**	
#1 Seed		*75%		25%		50%
#2 Seed		*75%		75%		25%
#3 Seed		100%		75%		25%
#4 Seed		75%		50%		50%
#5 Seed		100%		75%		0%
#6 Seed		75%		50%		0%
#7 Seed		75%		50%		50%
#8 Seed		50%		50%		25%
2nd Round Cells	**62.5%**		**37.5%**		**37.5%**	
Row #1		75%		50%		25%
Row #2		50%		0%		25%
Row #3 Cells		75%		25%		75%
Row #4		50%		50%		25%
3rd Round Cells	**50%**		**37.5%**		**75%**	
Row #1		50%		25%		50%
Row #2		50%		50%		100%
4th Round Cells	**25%**		**25%**		**50%**	
Row #1		25%		25%		50%
5th Round Cells	**100%**		**50%**		**50%**	
Row #1		100%		50%		50%
6th Round Cells	**100%**		**100%**		**100%**	
Row #1		100%		100%		100%

TABLE 6 (Continued)
2023 1st HALF BETTING STATISTICS BY ROUNDS

Round/Seed/Row	**Specific Rounds** Favorite **Money Line** Winning Percentage	**Seed or Row** Favorite **Money Line** Winning Percentage	**Specific Rounds** Favorite **Spread** Winning Percentage	**Seed or Row** Favorite **Spread** Covering Percentage	**Specific Rounds** Complete-game Total Overs	**Seed or Row** Over Winning Percentage
1st Round Cells	**68.75%**		**43.75%**		**40.6%**	
#1 Seed		*75%		25%		50%
#2 Seed		*75%		75%		75%
#3 Seed		100%		50%		75%
#4 Seed		75%		75%		25%
#5 Seed		75%		25%		0%
#6 Seed		50%		25%		50%
#7 Seed		25%		25%		50%
#8 Seed		75%		75%		0%
2nd Round Cells	**50%**		**37.5%**		**31.25%**	
Row #1		75%		50%		25%
Row #2		50%		50%		25%
Row #3		25%		25%		25%
Row #4		50%		25%		50%,
3rd Round Cells	**50%**		**37.5%**		**62.5%**	
Row #1		50%		50%		50%
Row #2		50%		50%		75%
4th Round Cells	**50%**		**75%**		**50%**	
Row #1		50%		75%		50%
5th Round Cells	**50%**		**50%**		**50%**	
Row #1		50%		50%		50%
6th Round Cells	**100%**		**100%**		**0%**	
Row #1		100%		100%		0%

Green highlighted numbers show potentially strong positive trends for the money line and spread of favorite teams.

Red highlighted numbers indicate a potentially strong trend for a money line or spread for dogs.

Yellow highlighted numbers mark potential trends for betting on the Total going under.

Blue highlighted numbers mark potential trends for betting on the Total going over.

*Indicates cells not highlighted because the odds are so unfavorable that the probability does not present a strong trend for wagering, e.g., a 75% probability for -10000 odds having a very small payoff.

Rows after the Third Round are not highlighted in recognition of sampling error.

Round/Seed/Row	**Specific Rounds** Favorite **Money Line** Winning Percentage	**Seed or Row** Favorite **Money Line** Winning Percentage	**Specific Rounds** Favorite **Spread** Winning Percentage	**Seed or Row** Favorite **Spread** Covering Percentage	**Specific Rounds** Complete-game Total Overs	**Seed or Row Over** Winning Percentage
1st Round Cells	**71.9%**		**50%**		**50%**	
#1 Seed		*100%		50%		50%
#2 Seed		*75%		50%		75%
#3 Seed		100%		100%		50%
#4 Seed		100%		25%		25%
#5 Seed		50%		50%		75%
#6 Seed		50%		50%		25%
#7 Seed		75%		25%		50%
#8 Seed		50%		50%		50%
2nd Round Cells	**68.8%**		**37.5%**		**56.25%**	
Row #1		75%		0%		100%
Row #2		50%		50%		50%
Row #3		50%		25%		50%
Row #4		100%		75%		25%
3rd Round Cells	**37.5%**		**25%**		**12.5%**	
Row #1		25%		0%		0%
Row #2		50%		50%		25%
4th Round Cells	**75%**		**75%**		**0%**	
Row #1		75%		75%		0%
5th Round Cells	**50%**		**50%**		**100%**	
Row #1		50%		50%		100%
6th Round Cells	**100%**		**0%**		**0%**	
Row #1		100%		0%		0%

Round/Seed/Row	Specific Rounds Favorite **Money Line** Winning Percentage	Seed or Row Favorite **Money Line** Winning Percentage	Specific Rounds Favorite **Spread** Winning Percentage	Seed or Row Favorite **Spread** Covering Percentage	Specific Rounds Complete-game Total Overs	Seed or Row Over Winning Percentage
1st Round Cells	65.6%		37.5%		37.5%	
#1 Seed		*100%		50%		0%
#2 Seed		*100%		50%		50%
#3 Seed		100%		75%		75%
#4 Seed		25%		25%		25%
#5 Seed		75%		0%		0%
#6 Seed		25%		25%		50%
#7 Seed		25%		0%		25%
#8 Seed		75%		75%		50%
2nd Round Cells	68.75%		50%		56.25%	
Row #1		50%		0%		75%
Row #2		50%		50%		50%
Row #3		75%		50%		50%
Row #4		100%		100%		50%
3rd Round Cells	75%		50%		0%	
Row #1		50%		50%		0%
Row #2		100%		75%		0%
4th Round Cells	50%		50%		25%	
Row #1		50%		50%		25%
5th Round Cells	100%	`	100%		50%	
Row #1		100%		100%		50%
6th Round Cells	0%		0%		0%	
Row #1		0%		0%		0%

Green highlighted numbers show potentially strong positive trends for the money line and spread of favorite teams.
Red highlighted numbers indicate a potentially strong trend for a money line or spread for dogs.
Yellow highlighted numbers mark potential trends for betting on the Total going under.
Blue highlighted numbers mark potential trends for betting on the Total going over.
*Indicates cells not highlighted because the odds are so unfavorable that the probability does not present a strong trend for wagering, e.g., a 75% probability for -10000 odds having a very small payoff.

Rows after the Third Round are not highlighted in recognition of sampling error.

PAPERS TO FACILITATE WAGERING

This book functions as a workbook that allows the gambler to use the historical data in Appendix A as a guide to generate the necessary information in Appendix B. This is to successfully produce documents to inform betting on the 2025 Tournament. To facilitate this, multiple documents are described and offered in the Appendices, which are:

- A House-generated Betting Sheet;
- Gambler-produced Bracket Matrix Charts;
- Gambler-created Parlay Building Block Sheets;
- Gambler-generated Regional Bracket Charts, and;
- Gambler-drafted Blank Bet Sheets.

HOUSE BETTING SHEETS

House betting sheets provided by the various sportsbooks show the betting options for the entire game of each contest in a Tournament round. Sometimes, these sheets present both full-game and half-time wagering information. The gambler should try to obtain sheets with complete-game and half-time betting to keep options open (See Sample Betting Sheet, Appendix A, pages 71 and 72). This sometimes requires obtaining two separate betting sheets from the House.

There are 32 first-round games with 64 teams to evaluate, so there is a lot of ground to cover. The sheer enormity of the possible bets means the House has less of an advantage over those wagering than in a typical situation. Therefore, the discerning gambler should be able to put together some winning tickets starting with a betting sheet review and the knowledge of this book. This process of reviewing a betting sheet in the First Round is facilitated by having a matrix chart (discussed below) provided in Appendix B of this book. This document can be filled out by the gambler to convert the data from the House bet sheet to the much more useful information in the matrix chart.

If a first-round matrix chart has already been created by the gambler prior to arriving at the sportsbook, e.g., getting the opening numbers from a sports betting app, the betting sheets from the House can be used to confirm the numbers on your matrix chart.

Confirmation of bet sheet information on the matrix chart with the actual odds on the House bet sheet is advised because the opening lines are subject to change. The result is the odds numbers that you receive on your bet tickets may not match the bet sheet exactly.

Ordinarily, this is not an issue, as it only slightly affects the ticket payout. But if you are betting on a team that changes from a dog to a favorite or vice versa, this may be a problem. For example, if you intend to bet on a team with a +1 spread with the actual number that you receive on the ticket being -1½ because the House has moved the odds, a team so affected could end up winning by 1 point but losing with respect to your wager. A cure here would be to take the team's money line. This would only change the odds from -110 to around -125. This is cheap insurance to avoid a loss (See Table 1, page 14). The odds on a bet sheet can also change by the time you actually wager, so check your odds, preferably at the window, if the spread is close to flipping.

Bracket Matrix Charts have already been generally introduced in the discussion of the analysis of gambling trends and directly above in connection with the House Betting Sheets. There are six matrix charts that together organize wagering information for each round of the Tournament. A first-round bracket matrix chart is on two pages because there are so many games to provide information on. The first page is a basic display of the matchup of teams with room in the matrix cells to print or write in the first half and final scores spreads and totals of the games (See Appendix A, pages 73 and 74 and Appendix B, pages 89 and 90).

The second page of the first-round matrix charts is more detailed, including all of the betting options and the time of the game. The matrix cells for games involving the #5 through the #8 seeds have a shaded background, recognizing how uncertain it is to determine wagering outcomes in these matchups. Charts for subsequent Tournament rounds are more concentrated with information. The cell information for matrix charts for the first and all subsequent rounds of the Tournament is formatted according to Figures 4 and 5 below.

Figure 4

READING A MATRIX CELL: 1st ROUND Sample Cell 2, 2, (See page 74)

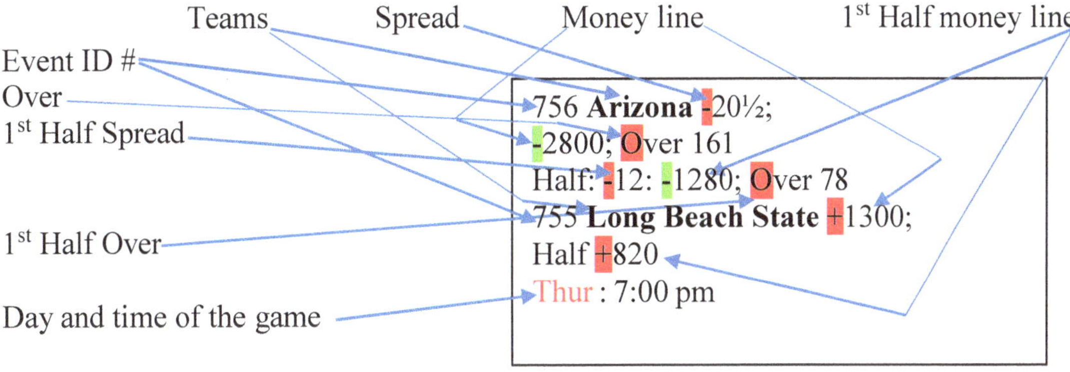

For the First Round of the Tournament, a cell in the matrix is identified by two numbers. The first number from left to right on the chart, excluding the first column of the chart, which indicates the seeding of the teams, indicates the column on the chart. The second number from top to bottom is the row of the chart. The information on the teams, spreads, money lines, and Totals of the contests within a cell is indicated by arrows (See Figure 4 above). The score is not shown in the actual cells of the First-round Detailed Matrix Chart, as that information is on the First-round Basic Bracket Matrix Chart.

Wagering results are noted by a red or green highlight over the specific bet option. A green highlight means that the betting option won. A red highlight means that the betting option lost. Figure 4 shows that Arizona did not cover for the entire game or at the half but did win both money line bets. The Total for the complete-game and at the Half was an under.

READING A MATRIX CELL: 3rd ROUND Sample Cell 2, 2; (See page 76)

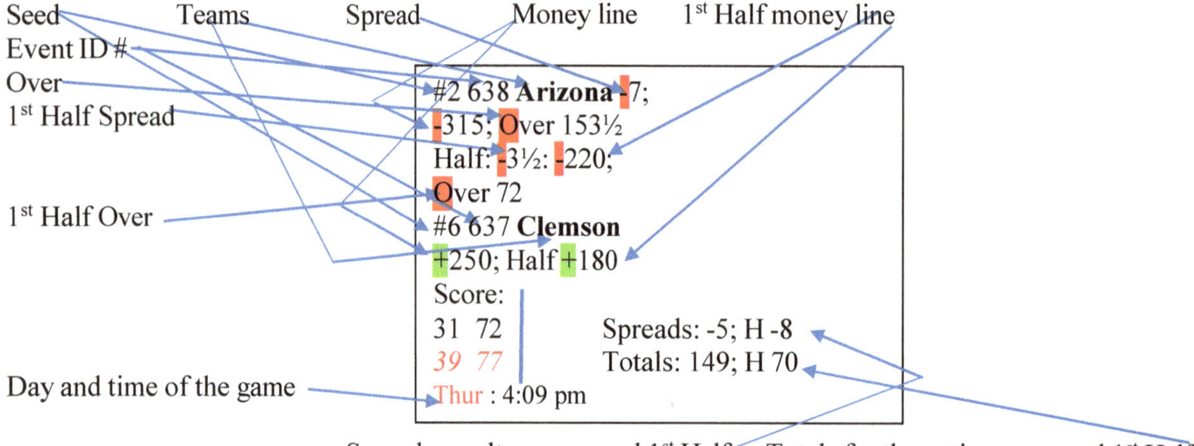

Spreads results, game, and 1st Half   Totals for the entire game and 1st Half

After Round One, the first number of a matrix cell from left to right is the column, and the second number from top to bottom is the row. The information on the teams, spreads, money lines, and Totals of the contests within a cell is indicated by arrows (See Figure 5 above). The score is shown for the first half and the game with the dog, which is not necessarily the higher seed, in italics. A red number indicates the dog being ahead of the favorite at that portion of the game. The spread and Total results are shown for the entire game first and then for the first half of the game.

As in round one, the results of the games are noted in the matrix cells by a red or green highlight over the specific bet options. A green highlight means that the betting option won. A red highlight means that the betting option lost, e.g., in Figure 5, the lower seed Arizona lost on the money line and spread for the half and the game with Totals that were both under. The matrix charts for the later rounds are on one page, continuing to show the seeding information. (See Appendix A, Tournament Matrix Charts, pages 73-78). This system clearly shows the progression of dogs through the rounds, indicating when upsets have occurred.

In any event, these matrix charts arguably assemble betting data into much more usable information than sportsbook betting sheets provide. But the matrix format is probably most effective in the first three rounds, where the greatest number of games are played and the most betting information is generated. A matrix chart can be used to create a parlay building block sheet (defined below) or lead directly to the creation of betting sheets (See Figure 7, page 52).

USE OF MATRIX CHARTS TO CREATE BET SHEETS

A matrix chart for any Tournament round may be used to establish which bets are going to be placed with the House. This can be done using different levels of sophistication, including:
- Subjective analysis of matrix cells;
- Selection of a matrix pattern on the chart followed by choosing bets within the cells, and;
- Semi-random selection of bets to various degrees with the aid of dice.

SUBJECTIVE MATRIX CELL ANALYSIS

More sophisticated gamblers can assemble bet sheets with this book's strategies by examining each cell of a matrix chart for a promising bet for the entire game or the first half. This bet can be for a dog, a favorite, or a Total. When a desired number of contests is identified, a bet ticket, whether it is an individual bet or a parlay, is formed.

SELECTION OF MATRIX PATTERNS

With this more casual method for selecting bets, the gambler can let chance be their guide by picking patterns of matrix cells for any Tournament round. This can be done without initially using any knowledge of basketball to create possible bets. These patterns may include diagonals, L-shapes, rows, columns, etc. Seven potential patterns to determine contests to include on a bet are identified in Figure 6, Selection of Parlay Bets Via Matrix Cell Patterns, page 45. These patterns can be established for any of the matrix charts for the Tournament Rounds in Appendix B. However, the gambler still must decide on the specific bets to make within each cell that is selected. This can be done subjectively once the cells are chosen or with the aid of dice, which is described below (See Table 7, row 4 for the column representing the Round that is involved).

SEMI-RANDOM SELECTION OF BETS

The semi-random selection of bets recognizes that many Tournament gamblers do not have sufficient experience to make bets with confidence. If this is the case, the gambler can resort to the use of dice to aid or totally determine wagering decisions. The assistance of dice is guided by this book, tailoring the probabilities of specific numbers appearing on the dice to the probabilities of winning outcomes. This results in the creation of Dice Intelligence "D I." For example, more dice combinations are interpreted to select the contest involving #3 seeds than bets involving #7 seeds. Thus, random dice results are purposely skewed to reflect more likely winning outcomes while allowing any bet to still be possible. The suggested manner in which the dice are used changes slightly for the rounds of the Tournament. Gamblers can also adapt their response to dice numbers to their style of wagering by making custom changes to the directions of Table 7 as explained below.

CHOOSING THE NUMBER OF EVENTS TO BET ON

A gambler can subjectively decide on the number of teams to use in a bet, or let dice make this determination. To semi-randomly make this decision, the gambler can roll a single die, e.g., a six would represent a six-team parlay. As an alternative, the dice can be rolled with the lower die number selecting the number of events on the parlay unless it is a one, in which case the higher die determines the number of parlay legs but with a tie of two ones or two sixes indicating an individual bet instead of a parlay and with any other tie signaling agreement for a parlay of that number. For example, if a four and a three are displayed on the dice, a three-team parlay would be indicated.

SELECTION OF FIRST-ROUND PARLAY BETS VIA MATRIX CELL PATTERNS
FOR 2024
(See 1st Round 2024 Basic Matrix Chart on page 73)

7-team parlay with cells containing favorites: UConn, Arizona, Kentucky, Alabama, Wisconsin, South Carolina, and Florida

3-team parlay with cells containing favorites: Purdue, Tennessee, and Michigan State

3-team parlay with cells containing favorites: Illinois, Saint Mary's, and Kansas

3-team parlay with cells containing favorites: Baylor, Auburn, San Diego State

3-team parlay with cells containing favorites: BYU, Duke, Creighton

3-team parlay with cells containing favorites: Texas Tech, Gonzaga, and Texas

4-team parlay with favorites: Washington State, Clemson, Dayton, Utah State

FIRST ROUND SEMI-RANDOM SELECTION OF BETS

DETERMINATION OF A MATRIX COLUMN

Each leg of a bet (an individual bet only has one leg) can be made by rolling a single die to establish a column. The number on the die represents the column number, except that the numbers five and six cancel the roll, which is then repeated to establish the column.

DETERMINATION OF A MATRIX ROW

The next step in assembling an individual bet leg is to roll a red and a green die. The number shown by the dice corresponds to the same row number of the matrix. The exceptions are that the dice displaying three and four calls for row #3; double fours choose row #4; display of a two and a six or double sixes signals row #1; the number nine selects row #2. And ten and eleven represent row #3. Once this step is completed, a cell on the matrix is identified.

SELECTION OF THE PORTION OF THE EVENT TO BET ON WITHIN A MATRIX CELL

With the row and column determined, the question is what bet is to be selected within the cell. With semi-random selection this is done with dice. Dice are rolled with the green die representing the entire game and the red die indicating the selection of the first half. The highest number of the die is the selected option. A "tie" of the die can go to the entire game to inject bias in that direction. Additional bias can be injected either toward the entire game or the half by lowering the rolled number on either die actually displayed by one, referred to in this book as "loading the dice." To illustrate, if the red die is a four, it could be considered to be a three, making it more likely that the number on the green die, representing the entire game, is higher than the red die.

Once the portion of the game is set by the above method, the gambler can either subjectively decide on the type of bet to make or rely further on the semi-random approach for the selection of the specific bet. If dice are used, the dice can be rolled with green representing the favorite and red representing the dog. The higher number of the dies determines the use of the favorite or dog. If the dice have the same number, a "tie" can go to the favorite or the dog at the gambler's option, as bias in that direction. Additional bias can be injected either toward the favorite or the dog by the gambler, lowering the rolled number on either die actually displayed by 1. However, in the First Round, favorite bias is more in line with statistics (See Table 6, Game Betting Statistics by Rounds, pages 35-40).

To determine the specific bet to select with dice, a green or red die is rolled depending on whether a favorite or dog has already been selected by the dice. For the green die, a #1, #2, or #3 signals a money line, while a #4 or #5 roll calls for a spread, and a #6 indicates a Total. For a red die, a #1, #2, #3, or #4 signals a spread, while a roll of a #5 calls for a money line, and a #6 indicates a Total. In the event of a #6 for a green or red die, a final roll of the dice is required, with the green die for the over and the red die for the under. The highest number on these dice determines the under or over, and a tie gives the nod to the **under**. The entire first-round process is repeated until the desired number of bet legs is selected.

SECOND ROUND SEMI-RANDOM SELECTION OF BETS

DETERMINATION OF A MATRIX COLUMN

For the Second Round, again for each leg of a bet, a single die is rolled to establish a column with the number on the die corresponding to the same column number. The exception is that the numbers 5 and 6 invalidate the roll, which is then repeated to establish the column.

DETERMINATION OF A MATRIX ROW

Next, one die is rolled to select a row of the matrix. The number shown on that die corresponds to the same row number of the matrix, except that the numbers 5 and 6 invalidate the roll, which is then repeated to establish a valid row. With the selection of a column and row, a matrix cell is located.

SELECTION OF THE TYPE OF BET WITHIN A MATRIX CELL

With the row and column determined for the Second Round, dice can be rolled with the green die representing the entire game and the red die designating the first half. The highest number of the die is the selected option. A "tie" of the die can go to a selection of the entire game to inject bias in that direction.

Once the portion of the game is set, the dice can be rolled with green representing the favorite and red representing the dog. The higher number of the dies determines the use of the favorite or dog. If the die has the same number, bias can go toward the favorite to most closely model trends of the Tournament.

To select a specific bet within a matrix cell, a green or red die is rolled depending on whether a favorite or dog has been determined by the dice. For the green die, a #1, #2, #3, or #4 signals a money line, while a #5 roll calls for a spread and a #6 indicates a Total. For a red die, a #1, #2, or #3 signals a spread, while a #4 or a #5 roll calls for a money line, and a #6 indicates a Total. In the event of a #6 for a green or red die, selecting a Total, a final roll of the dice is required with the green die for the over and the red die for the under. The highest number on these dies determines the under or over, and a tie gives the nod to the **under**.

THIRD ROUND SEMI-RANDOM SELECTION OF BETS

DETERMINATION OF A MATRIX COLUMN

In the Third Round, a semi-random bet can be set up by rolling one die to select a column with the number shown corresponding to the same column number. The exception is that the numbers 5 and 6 invalidate the roll, which is then repeated to establish the column.

DETERMINATION OF A MATRIX ROW

Next, a semi-random bet is set up by rolling one die to select a row of the matrix. Number 1, 2, and 3 signal row 1, die numbers 4, 5, and 6 correspond to row two.

SELECTION OF THE TYPE OF BET WITHIN A MATRIX CELL

With the row and column determined, a matrix cell is established. If the dice are used to choose the betting option for the selected cell, the dice are rolled with the green die representing the entire game and the red die representing the first half. The highest number of the die is the selected option. A "tie" of the die can go to a selection of the first half to inject a little bias in that direction.

Once the portion of the game is set, if the dice are to be used to determine the betting option, they can be rolled with green representing the favorite and red representing the dog. The higher number on the dies determines the use of the favorite or dog. If the dice have the same number, a "tie" can go to the dog as bias in that direction.

To select a specific bet within a matrix cell, a green or red die is rolled depending on whether a favorite or dog has been determined by the dice. For the green die, a #1, #2, #3, or #4 signals a money line, while a roll of #5 calls for a spread, and a #6 indicates a Total. For a red die, a #1, #2, or #3 signals a spread, while a #4 or #5 roll calls for a money line, and a #6 indicates a Total. In the event of a #6 for a green or red die selecting a Total, a final roll of the dice is required with the green die for the over and the red die for the under. The highest number on these dies determines the under or over, and a tie gives the nod to the **over**.

SEMI-RANDOM BET SELECTION FOR THE LAST THREE ROUNDS OF THE TOURNAMENT

After the Third Round, betting choices are limited to the point that a semi-random pick of a matrix cell may not be helpful. However, if a cell is subjectively picked with dice following the Third Round, the bet within that cell can be established with the semi-random system described in Table 7, Semi-random Selection of Bets by Rounds, pages 49 and 50.

PARLAY BUILDING BLOCK SHEETS

In the First Round, the Parlay Building Block Sheet lists all teams in the Tournament with columns to speculate yes or no on the betting prospects of each team with regard to winning the money line for the complete-game, winning the first-half money line, covering the spread for the game, covering the first-half spread, and deciding whether the game and first-half Total will be an over.

TABLE 7
SEMI-RANDOM SELECTION OF BETS BY ROUNDS
(first three rounds)

Decision to be made	**First** Round	**Second** Round	**Third** Round
Number of Events on the Bet Ticket Using Dice	Roll the **dice**, a tie, or the lower # on the **die** represents the # of events on the bet ticket.	Roll the **dice**, a tie, or the lower # on the **die** represents the # of events on the bet ticket.	Roll the **dice**, a tie, or the lower # on the **die** represents the # of events on the bet ticket.
Determination of the Matrix **Column**	Roll one **die** representing the **column** except **die #**s 5 or 6 means that the roll is repeated.	Roll one **die** representing the **column** except **die #**s 5 or 6 means that the roll is repeated.	Roll one **die** representing the **column** except **die #**s 5 or 6 means that the roll is repeated.
Determination of the Matrix **Row**	The **dice** number represents the **row,** except the display of three and four calls for row #3; double fours choose row #4; display of a two and a six or double sixes signals row #1; the number nine selects row #2. The numbers ten and eleven pick row #3.	Roll a **die** with the # corresponding to the matrix row, except die #s 5 and 6 means that the roll is repeated.	Roll a **die** with the numbers 1, 2, and 3 representing row 1 and the numbers 4, 5, and 6 selecting row 2.
Selection of the **Entire Game** or **Halftime**	Read the red **die** minus 1 with a higher # or tie on the green **die** choosing the **entire game.**	Read the red **die** minus 1 with a higher # or tie on the green **die** choosing the **entire game.**	Roll the **dice** with a higher # or tie on the red **die,** choosing the **halftime.**
Choice of the **Favorite** (green die) or **Dog** (Red die)	Read the red die minus 1 with a tie or the higher # on the green **die,** selecting the **favorite**.	Roll the **dice** with a tie or the higher # on the green **die,** selecting the **favorite**.	Roll the **dice** with a tie or the higher # on the red **die,** selecting the **dog**.
Selection of the Specific Bet with the **Green** Die	A roll of 1, 2, 3, or 4 signals a **money line**; 5 calls for a **spread**; and 6 indicates a **Total,** as determined below.	A roll of a 1, 2, 3, or 4 signals a **money line**; a 5 calls for a **spread**; and a 6 indicates a **Total** as determined below.	A roll of a 1, 2, or 3 signals a **money line**; a 4 or 5 calls for a **spread**; and a 6 indicates a **Total** as determined below.
Selection of the Specific Bet with the **Red** Die	A roll of 1, 2, 3, or 4 signals a **spread**; 5 calls for a **money line,** and a 6 indicates a **Total,** as determined below.	A roll of a 1, 2, or 3 signals a **spread**; a 4 or 5 calls for a **money line,** and a 6 indicates a **Total** as determined below.	A roll of 1, 2, or 3 signals a **spread**; 4 or 5 calls for a **money line,** and a 6 indicates a **Total** as determined below.
Determination of a **Total** with dice	Reading the green die minus 1 with a tie or the higher # on the red **die,** selecting the **under.**	Reading the green die minus 1 with a tie or the higher # on the red **die,** selecting the **under.**	Roll the dice with a tie or the higher # on the green **die,** selecting the **over.**

49

SEMI-RANDOM SELECTION OF BETS BY ROUNDS

(last three rounds)

Decision to be made	**Fourth** Round	**Fifth** Round	**Sixth** Round
Number of Events on the Bet Ticket Using Dice	N/A, a subjective decision is most reasonable.	N/A, a subjective decision is most reasonable.	N/A, a subjective decision is most reasonable.
Determination of the Matrix **Column**	Roll one **die** representing the **column** except **die** #s 5 or 6 means that the roll is repeated.	Roll one **die** with 1, 2, and 3 representing **column** 1; otherwise, **column** 2 is selected.	There is only one **column**.
Determination of the Matrix **Row**	There is only one row.	There is only one row.	There is only one row.
Selection of the **Entire Game** or **Halftime**	Roll the **dice** with a higher # or tie on the **red die,** choosing the **halftime**	Roll the **dice** with a higher # or tie on the **green die,** choosing the **entire game**	Roll the **dice** with a higher # or tie on the **green die,** choosing the **entire game**
Choice of the **Favorite** (green die) or **Dog** (Red die)	Roll the **dice** with a tie or the higher # on the **green die,** selecting the **favorite.**	Roll the **dice** with a tie or the higher # on the **green die,** selecting the **favorite.**	Roll the **dice** with a tie or the higher # on the **green die,** selecting the **favorite.**
Selection of the Specific Bet with the **Green** Die	A roll of a 1, 2, 3, or 4 signals a **money line**; a 5 calls for a **spread**; and a 6 indicates a **Total** as determined below.	A roll of 1, 2, or 3 signals a **money line**; 4 or 5 calls for a **spread**; and 6 indicates a **Total,** as determined below.	A roll of 1, 2, or 3 signals a **money line**; 4 or 5 calls for a **spread**; and 6 indicates a **Total,** as determined below.
Selection of the Specific Bet with the **Red** Die	A roll of a 1, 2, 3, or 4 signals a **spread**; a 5 calls for a **money line,** and a 6 indicates a **Total,** as determined below.	A roll of 1, 2, 3, or 4 signals a **spread**; a 5 calls for a **money line,** and a 6 indicates a **Total,** as determined below.	A roll of 1, 2, 3, or 4 signals a **spread**; a 5 calls for a **money line,** and a 6 indicates a **Total,** as determined below.
Determination of a **Total** with dice	Roll the dice with a tie or the higher # on the **green die,** selecting the **over.**	Roll the dice with a tie or the higher # on the **green die,** selecting the **over.**	Roll the dice with the tie or the higher # on the **red die,** selecting the **under.**

Parlay building block charts change as the Tournament progresses. The chart for the First Round lists all 68 teams and can be helpful when coordinated with the First-round Matrix Chart and First-round Betting Sheet. As the rounds progress, the list of teams on the parlay building block sheets shrinks quickly, reducing to 32 teams in the Second Round, 16 teams in the Third Round, 8 teams in the Fourth Round, and finally 2 in the Sixth Round. Therefore, the gambler can decide if and when these sheets are no longer useful. Be aware that the team numbers change each round! For example, the event identification number for North Carolina State in the Third Round of the Tournament was 643 but changed to 657 for their fourth-round game.

It should be clear that it is not necessary to fill out all or any of the cells of the parlay building block sheet. The point is to have a sheet where teams can be quickly identified in alphabetical order, displaying their universal betting numbers with a row of cells to catalog and customize information for the assembly of potential bets.

BETTING SHEETS

From selections of games highlighted on a matrix chart or cataloged on the parlay building block sheet, various individual and parlay bets can be assembled. The blank parlay betting sheets make it possible to physically write out potential bets and have cells to write in the payoff of these bets at various wagering levels. Once satisfied with bets, e.g., after planning wagers on scratch paper, the gambler can use a final version of a betting sheet to order at the House betting window.

During the assembly of parlay betting sheets, the gambler should be aware of the number of times an outcome is being bet on. For example, if an outcome is used three times on ten bet tickets and the wager loses, 30% of your bet tickets are in the trash! Well-reasoned use of hedge betting may soften the blow of losses on a "can't miss" team that is used multiple times (See page 25).

REGIONAL BRACKET SHEETS

The regional bracket sheet is simply another way of getting a picture of how the Tournament is progressing (See Regional Bracket Sheets pages 85 and 86 as templates for pages 107 and 108). If the outcomes of games are being charted as results come in, future matchups can be anticipated, and parlay bets can be reloaded when losses are sustained.

SUMMARY OF THE USE OF ANALYSIS SHEETS AND CHARTS

The most comprehensive practice to organize your wagering is to review the forms provided in Appendix A, documenting 2024 results as a guide to fill out the 2025 forms in Appendix B. This starts with the First Round by filling out the bracket matrix chart. The process can begin immediately after Selection Sunday in 2025, when the 68-team Tournament field is announced.

Next, actual spread and odds information will become quickly available at online gambling sites. The gambler is advised to look at an internet site such as www.scoresandodds.com or www.vsin.com, that provides universally accepted betting numbers with the names of the teams, e.g., 841 for Duke. This is so that you are ready to wager whether a sportsbook uses numbers or names to take bets. At this stage, the matrix for the 64-team field is not completely set, as the First Four games to eliminate four teams have not been contested.

When you arrive at the sportsbook, confirm the odds on your matrix chart with the House Betting Sheet, fill out a Parlay Building Block Sheet as desired, assemble tentative bet tickets by reference to the matrix chart and parlay building block sheet, reconsider potential bets by checking injury reports (See below) and the payout potential of the bets using a parlay calculator provided by many on-line gambling sites. And finally make your wagers with the House (See Figure 7, Coordination of Bet Analysis Documents, page 52).

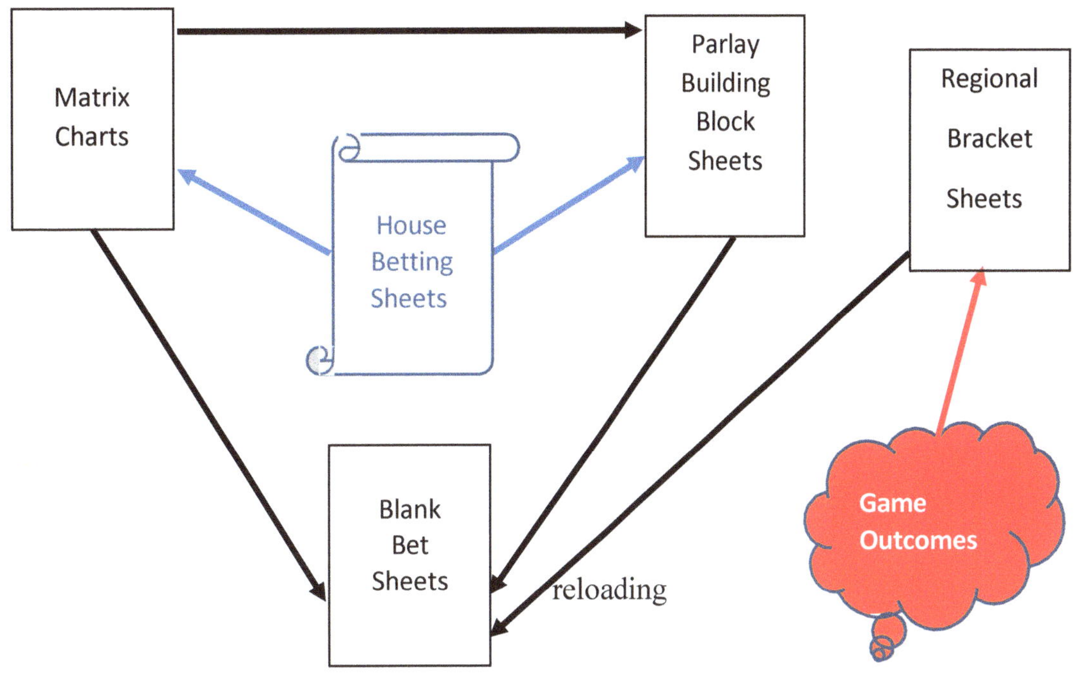

For each round, a House betting sheet can be used to create a matrix chart for ease of information evaluation. This matrix chart can be used to create parlay building block sheets or lead directly to the creation of betting tickets for each Tournament round.

In the process of deciding which teams to bet on, the gambler is free to and is encouraged to customize the use of the above documents combined with the strategies illuminated in the book to fit their personal betting style. This includes consideration of the amounts to wager, the sophistication of data analysis, the risks and rewards of specific bets, and preferences toward wagering on favorites or dogs.

SCORING STATISTICS

To aid in betting decisions, the gambler can utilize the statistical information provided through the book's email, which may not be active for the 2025 Tournament but is hoped to be available at the gambler's request after Selection Sunday at beatingtheoddsofmarch@yahoo.com. If the statistics are available, they will be received by the gambler as an attachment under the email signature Alan Sheats. The overall intent of these statistics is to downplay much of the data of questionable relevance from other sources that gamblers frequently rely on. Here, the focus is on statistical information about how teams have performed during the regular season against opponents that are now actually in the Tournament-separating the wheat from the chaff (See the match-up between Purdue v. Gonzaga, Figure 8, Team Scoring Data Sheets, page 53 and 54).

Figure 8
TEAM SCORING DATA SHEET

PURDUE (2024 Midwest Regional #1 seed)

Date Game was played (**H** indicates a home game)	Opponent (black indicates Opponent is in Tournament)	1st Half **Team/opponent** Team Scores; [Spread]; (*Total*)	2nd Half **Team/opponent** Scores; {Spread}	Full Game **Team/opponent** Spread/ Total (- indicates A loss)	Overtime **Team/ opponent** Team scores for each overtime; (Spread)
11/6/2023 H	Samford	51/17 [34] 68	47/28 {19}	98-45 (53) 143	
11/10/2023 H	Morehead St.	42/29 [13] **71**	45/28 {17}	87-57 (30) **144**	
11/13/2023 H	Xavier	37/29 [8] 66	46/42 {4}	83-71 (12) 154	
11/20/2023 H	Gonzaga	30/35 [-5] **65**	43/28 {15}	73-63 (10) **136**	
11/21/2023 H	Tennessee	30/31 [-1] **61**	41/36 {5}	71-67 (4) **138**	
11/22/2023	Marquette	45/33 [12] **78**	33/42 {-9}	78-75 (3) **153**	
11/28/2023	TX Southern	44/29 [15] 73	55/38 {17}	99-67 (32) 166	
12/1/2022 H	Northwestern	40/32 [8] **72**	36/44 {-8}	88-92 (-4) **180**	12-16 (-4)
12/4/2023 H	Iowa	45/24 [21] 69	42/44 {-2}	87-68 (19) 155	
12/9/2023	Alabama	47/49 [-2] **96**	45/37 {8}	92-86 (6) **178**	
12/16/2023 H	Arizona	49/38 [11] **87**	43/46 {-3}	92-84 (8) **176**	
12/21/2023 H	Jacksonville	45/27 [18] 72	55/30 {15}	100-57 (43) 157	
12/29/2023	E. Kentucky	43/24 [9] 67	37/29 {8}	80-53 (27) 133	
1/2/2024 H	Maryland	32/19 [13] 51	35/34 {-1}	67-53 (14) 120	
1/5/2024H	Illinois	47/32 [15] **79**	36/46 {-10}	83-78 (5) **161**	
1/9/2024 H	Nebraska	30/41 [-11] **71**	42/47 {-5}	72-88 (-16) **160**	
1/13/2024 H	Penn St.	56/36 [20] 92	39/42 {-3}	95-78 (17) 173	
1/16/2024 H	Indiana	51/29 [22] **80**	36/37 {-1}	87-66 (21) **153**	
1/20/2024 H	Iowa	47/34 [13] **81**	37/36 {1}	84-70 (14) **154**	
1/23/2024	Michigan	49/25 [24] 74	50/42 {8}	99-67 (32) 166	
1/28/2024	Rutgers	33/20 [13] 53	35/40 {-5}	68-60 (8) 128	
1/31/2024 H	Northwestern	47/39 [8] **86**	34/42 {-8}	105-96 (9) **201**	24-15 (9)
2/4/2024 H	Wisconsin	32/34 [-2] **66**	37/41 {-4}	69-75 (-6) **144**	
2/10/2024	Indiana	37/25 [12] **62**	42/34 {8}	79-59 (20) 138	
2/15/2024	Minnesota	35/43 [-8] 78	49/33 {16}	84-76 (8) 160	
2/18/2024 H	Ohio St.	30/35 [-5] 65	39/38 {1}	69-73 (-4) 142	
2/22/2024 H	Rutgers	52/33 [19] 85	44/35 {9}	96-68 (28) 164	
2/25/2024 H	Michigan	47/36 [11] 83	37/40 {-3}	84-76 (8) 160	
3/2/2024	Michigan St.	38/35 [3] **73**	42/39 {3}	80-74 (6) **154**	
3/5/2024	Illinois	34/40 [-6] **74**	43/31 {12}	77-71 (6) **148**	
3/10/2024	Wisconsin	44/33 [11] **77**	34/37 {-3}	78-70 (8) **148**	

53

GONZAGA (2024 Midwest Regional #5 seed)

Date Game was played (**H** indicates a home game)	Opponent (black indicates Opponent is in Tournament)	1st Half **Team/opponent** Team Scores; [Spread]; (*Total*)	2nd Half **Team/opponent** Scores; {Spread}	Full Game **Team/opponent** Spread/ Total (- indicates A loss)	Overtime **Team/ opponent** Team scores for each overtime; (Spread)
11/10/2023 H	Yale	47/42 [5] 89	39/29 {10}	86-71 (15) 157	
11/14/2023 H	Eastern Oregon	63/30 [33] 93	60/27 {33}	123-57 (66) 180	
11/20/2023 H	Purdue	35/30 [5] **65**	28/43 {-15}	63-73 (-10) **136**	
11/28/2023 H	CSUB	44/29 [15] 73	37/36 {1}	81-65 (16) 146	
12/2/2023	USC	44/37 [7] 81	45/39 {6}	89-76 (13) 165	
12/5/2023 H	AR-Pine Bluff	59/30 [29] 89	52/41 {11}	111-71 (40) 182	
12/9/2023	Washington	48/42 [6] **90**	25/36 {-11}	73-78 (-5) **151**	
12/11/2022 H	MS Valley	38/18 [20] 56	40/22 {18}	78-40 (38) 118	
12/15/2023 H	UConn	34/45 [-11] **79**	29/31 {-2}	63-76 (-13) **139**	
12/20/2023 H	Jackson State	41/29 [12] 70	59/47 {12}	100-76 (24) 176	
12/29/2023 H	San Diego St.	37/38 [-1] **75**	37/46 {-9}	74-84 (-10) **158**	
1/4/2023 H	Pepperdine	45/27 [18] 72	41/33 {8}	86-60 (26) 146	
1/6/2023 H	San Diego	55/35 [20] 90	46/39 {7}	101-74 (27) 175	
1/11/2023	Santa Clara	34/40 [-6] 74	42/37 {5}	76-77 (-1) 153	
1/18/2024	Pepperdine	40/40 [0] 80	46/21 {25}	86-61 (25) 147	
1/20/2024	San Diego	54/27 [27] 81	51/36 {15}	105-63 (42) 168	
1/25/2024 H	San Francisco	30/31 [-1] 61	47/41 {6}	77-72 (5) 149	
1/27/2024	Pacific	34/35 [-1] 69	48/38 {10}	82-73 (9) 155	
1/30/2024 H	LMU	45/29 [16] 74	47/29 {18}	92-58 (34) 150	
2/3/2024 H	St. Mary's	34/33 [1] **67**	28/31 {-3}	62-64 (-2) **126**	
2/7/2024 H	Portland	50/23 [27] 73	46/41 {5}	96-64 (32) 160	
2/10/2024	Kentucky	42/32 [10] **74**	47/53 {-6}	89-85 (4) 174	
2/15/2024	LMU	47/46 [1] 93	44/28 {16}	91-74 (17) 165	
2/17/2024 H	Pacific	47/34 [13] 81	55/42 {13}	102-76 (26) 178	
2/22/2024	Portland	43/30 [13] 73	43/35 {8}	86-65 (21) 151	
2/24/2024 H	Santa Clara	52/46 [6] 98	42/35 {77}	94-81 (13) 175	
2/29/2024	San Francisco	35/34 [1] 69	51/34 {17}	86-68 (18) 154	
3/2/2024 H	St. Mary's	44/28 [16] **72**	26/29 {-3}	70-57 (13) **127**	

For gambling purposes, most Tournament games feature contests where the teams have not played each other during the year, nor have they faced many, if any, common opponents. Despite these major limitations on the predictability of the outcomes of events, each team in the Tournament has its own data sheet that has six categories which point out the following:

- Column 1—shows the date that a game was played, e.g., early or late in the season, and shows if this was a road game or was played at home, indicated by a (H).

- Column 2—indicates the quality of the opponent, noting whether they are in the Tournament. This is a measure of the value of the game information as a predictor of Tournament success for the team being analyzed. A team that is in the Tournament is in black. If the team in black was beaten by the team being examined, the defeated team is on a green background.

- Column 3—shows how many points the team scores and allows in the first half of each game. The first number is the score of the team being examined, and the second score is that of the opponent. The difference in the numbers is negative if the team being examined had fewer points at the half. This information can be used in betting the Tournament first-half money line, and first-half spread. For opponents in the Tournament, the first-half score is shown in *italics* to help predict Tournament first-half Totals.

- Column 4—demonstrates several aspects of a team's skills, including the ability to come from behind from a deficit in the first half, the propensity to play down to inferior competition, whether a team is satisfied with a lead or shows the killer instinct to pull away from a team that they have a lead on.

- Column 5–reflects information for the full game over and the full game spread. The numbers answer the question of whether a team pours it on throughout the game or allows an opponent to close at the end of the game by taking their "foot off the gas." This column shows the teams that are likely to win or lose the close games. Yellow highlights in this column indicate negative trends during the course of the regular season, such as prolonged stretches of losses.

- Column 6—demonstrates a team's propensity to get involved in overtime games and how a team handles the heightened intensity of an extra five-minute overtime session(s).

The example in figure 8, on pages 53 and 54, is the presentation of the data sheets for Purdue and Gonzaga. These are teams that met in the Third Round of the 2024 Tournament. A comparison of datasheets indicates that Purdue had an edge in this game, having won a head-to-head battle by ten points even though the contest was at Purdue and was way back at the beginning of the season on November 20, 2023. Purdue's obvious advantage with regard to the level of competition is shown by the fact that they had played fourteen games against teams also in the Tournament, winning all but one of those contests. Gonzaga, on the other hand, only played seven games with Tournament teams fairly early in the season mostly at home, losing all but two of those contests.

With a -4½ point spread and -210 money line for the complete-game of Purdue, either favorite bet was very attractive. The trends of the teams pointed to a first Over 74, with the complete-game history of the squads suggesting that the final score would be less than the 155-point Total (See the 4, 1 matrix cell in the 2024 NCAA Tournament 3rd Round Bracket Matrix Chart for the match-up of Purdue and Gonzaga on page 76).

By utilizing a regular season scoring sheet on all 68 teams in the Tournament, each game can be analyzed in a side-by-side comparison of the opponents, as has been done with Purdue and Gonzaga above.

PLAYER INJURIES

A key component of deciding on a potential bet is to check the injury report. The health of players is a very important part of evaluating spreads and odds assigned to a team regardless of the Tournament round as this relates to betting. For example, in 2022, the Achilles tendon tear sustained in the Third Round by a starting forward for Villanova signaled that their opponent, Kansas, was a predictable winner in their Final Four clash. Similarly, the injury to North Carolina's center in their semi-final game in 2022, which ultimately surfaced in earnest in the fourth quarter of the Championship game, was arguably the straw that allowed Kansas to break the Tar Heels' back and become the 2022 National Champion.

Information about injuries to college basketball players can be gained by watching the games and from sources such as www.covers.com, www.sportsdatausatoday, and www.rotowire.com.

TIME TO BET

It is best to start putting your tickets together as soon as the NCAA Tournament bracket is announced on Selection Sunday. There is a lot of information to go through to put together tickets with the best chance of winning. Online gambling sites are valuable at this stage as they post the tentative odds for the gambling options almost immediately after the teams are announced.

It is helpful to choose an internet site that includes the sportsbook team numbers for the first-round games. Otherwise, you may only have access to the names of the teams to set up bets and then may have to use the House betting sheets later to convert the names to the numbers that are the currency of placing bets at many of the sportsbooks. There is no point in doing this extra work! Putting together potential tickets before you travel to the sportsbook can avoid a lot of anxiety. You also should consider testing the payout of the tickets with an online parlay calculator, which incidentally works on an individual bet, to calculate a money line payoff. For example, this is to make sure that your five-team parlay doesn't require $25.00 to make $3.50.

When you arrive at a sportsbook, it is helpful to bet early for the First Round of the Tournament, definitely before the crush on Thursday, with the games beginning at 9:00 am. Nothing is worse than being in line to bet with someone at the window taking forever to make up their mind on which team to put $5.00 on when you have bets that include teams playing in games starting in a few minutes.

With regard to the odds on a particular game in the Tournament, the House establishes opening spreads and odds. These numbers change as bets are made, and the House balances the money. This balancing act is particularly difficult in the Tournament because of the large number of unsophisticated gamblers.

Therefore, an astute gambler can use this information in deciding how to bet. As a case in point, if you are considering a bet on an over and the number continues to move up, the consensus of the gamblers is that the House opening Total number is too low. The House is likely to actually be correct, and therefore, a bet on the under based on the new Total may be a reasonable wager.

Generally, in the Tournament, it is best to bet early on favorites before the numbers become unfavorable and bet late on the dogs for more attractive odds. However, with all the planning in the world, it should be remembered that because of the chaos of the first-day betting frenzy and the unpredictability of college basketball generally, you need to be ready to place bets anytime during the days of the Tournament as results come in. You need to be flexible!

PLACING BETS

At the point of being ready to bet, you have probably massaged a lot of information, and it's time to communicate your wagers to the House. This is done either by contact with the ticket takers of the sportsbook or by use of a kiosk (automated ticket dispensing machines). With direct contact with a ticket taker, remember that some sportsbooks use the actual names of the teams to take bets, while to the ticket takers at other sportsbooks, your bet is just a number. This means that you may be able to say "straight" (individual) bet on Kentucky, the money line, for $20, or you may have to say something like "721" (we do not know the actual number) the money line for $20. Similarly, if a bet was placed at a sportsbook using numbers by saying "1721 the over for $20", this is a first-half bet on the over in the Kentucky game, with the request of the first half indicated by the 1 in front of the 721 universal betting number.

When ordering a parlay, the number or the name of a team involved is stated first. For instance, "I have a three-team parlay, 734 (Kentucky), the spread, 764 (Texas), the spread, and 772 (Ohio State) the over for $20". The name or number associated with the team may not need to be given to the ticket-taker, depending on the House you are dealing with.

When placing multiple bets, precision is helpful to avoid mistakes on tickets and not waste time, stressing yourself, the ticket-taker, and the gamblers behind you waiting to make their bets. It helps to place bets from a written "menu" that you create (See betting sheets). This scheme can be started with individual games progressing to more complex parlays. As one strategy with a House using numbers, each ticket can be requested according to ascending game numbers facilitating order, e.g., 733 (St. Peters), the spread); 766 (Purdue), the spread; 774 (Villanova), the money line for $15.

To eliminate the need for human contact to purchase bet tickets altogether, the gambler can frequently use ticket dispensing machines called "kiosks." These machines are specific to the various sportsbooks with different methods of operation that require some experience to gain proficiency. Universally, the kiosks are operated by touch screens with numerous sports icons that include basketball leagues from all over the world down to the more familiar American professional basketball and the college ranks of the Tournament that is the focus of Beating the Odds of March.

The kiosks provide the freedom to place bets even when the sportsbook is not open for regular service by ticket takers. Further, the machines allow the gambler to experiment with potential bets by making it possible to add and subtract parlay legs, and even move between sports. In the context of basketball, bets can be made from different tournaments, separated by divisions and even genders with relative ease and with the payout results instantly displayed. However, the gambler has to make sure that they are on the correct day and betting on the proper portion of the game that is being wagered on to produce an intended ticket. For example, if it is Wednesday, March 20,

2025, and the gambler selects the Tournament icon on the kiosk touch screen, and if the option for tomorrow's games is activated, the screen will not show Friday's contests. To display the Friday games, the machine would have to be set in the "upcoming" mode. The point is, the operation of the kiosk is not completely intuitive and sometimes the best practice is to talk to the sportsbook ticket taker about your bet if it is complicated.

In any event, arguably the greatest flexibility that the kiosk provides is the ability to place a bet on a contest that is in progress, referred to as "in-game wagering". This ability makes possible numerous new gambling opportunities, e.g., monitoring games where the favorite is behind at the beginning of the contest but is expected to recover by the game's end. In such a situation, the odds will improve for the favorite as they fall behind in the game, and if a bet on the favorite is placed at that time and the team later recovers, the gambler's payout can be significantly increased over the gambler that simply bet on the favorite before the game started.

The downside to this ability to bet on games in progress is the psychological tendency to chase and compound bad gambling decisions, e.g., betting in game to support a pre-game bet that is not going well. The gambler should remember that in this wagering on the fly, the House has the benefit of number crunching AI against the gambler's likely bias intuition.

To prepare the gambler for the placement of actual bets, sample bets for the 2024 Tournament, with explanations of why they were assembled and the outcomes of these contests, are provided below.

<h2 style="text-align:center">SAMPLE 2024 TOURNAMENT BETS</h2>

<h3 style="text-align:center">FIRST-ROUND SAMPLE BETS</h3>

Example #1 (three-team parlay)

- 726 North Carolina, -25.5; 796 Baylor, -510; 1741 Duquesne, +5

Bet of:	$10	$15	$20	$25	$30	$
Payout:	$33.59	$50.39	$67.19	$83.9	$100.78	

This three-team parlay was set up months before the teams were even announced on Selection Sunday for the 2024 Tournament. This was done by what the book calls a "Pre-pick, using the semi-random team selection system (See Table 7, column 2, page 49).

By rolling dice according to the direction of Table 7, bets for three matrix cells with specific seeds and regions were established. The cells and specific bets that were identified are column 2, row 2, a wager in the West Regional for the first-half spread for what turned out to be the #1 seed North Carolina. The second event was column 2, row 3, calling for the complete-game money line for the West Regional #3 seed, which turned out to be Baylor. Finally, a spread bet on the first half was made on what ended up being #11 seed Duquesne, in column 1, row 6, representing the East Regional.

58

After the Tournament teams were revealed on Selection Sunday, the result was a three-leg parlay win guided by the intelligent application of dice. This was all without having to know anything about college basketball! The pre-pick for the 2025 Tournament is provided in this book on page 111.

Example #2 (eight-team parlay)

- 1748 Iowa St., -610; 1756 Arizona -1280; 1767 Marquette -530; 1728Tennessee -910; 744 Illinois -865; 776 Baylor -1000; 736 Kentucky -1100; 740 Creighton -735

Bet of:	$10	$15	$20	$25	$30	$100
Payout:	$15.18	$22.77	$30.36	$37.95	$45.54	$151.79

Here, the strategy was to take into account the high first round money line winning percentages of the #2 and #3 seeds to put together an eight-team parlay using the four number two-seeds and the four three-seeds. The expectation was that none of the teams would lose in the first round. This is like filling out a "chalk" bracket in an office pool. The teams are easy to identify in the matrix format of this book. This is done by simply looking across the two and three-seed rows.

The plan was working to perfection until the collapse of Kentucky at the hands of Oakland, with the Wildcats trailing at the Half and at the end of the game. The "can't miss" ticket was a loser. The unexpected loss of Kentucky was magnified by the fact that the Wildcats were used on other parlay tickets. This illustrates the risk of using a team on multiple bet tickets. Of course, when a team is expected to win, there is an incentive to parlay that team in various scenarios on different bet tickets. The best one can do is at least know the financial risk posed by each team represented on your bet tickets and bet accordingly.

Example #3 (four-team parlay)

- 744 Illinois -865; 740 Creighton -735; 784 Alabama -510; 752 Kansas -220

Bet of:	$10	$15	$20	$25	$30	$
Payout:	$12.05	$18.07	$24.10	$30.12	$36.15	

In the First Round, two #3 seeds are paired with two #4 seeds. In the group, the money lines are fairly comparable with respect to the expected risk, with the exception of Kansas being projected by the sportsbooks as significantly riskier than the other teams. This bet was made purposefully to recognize that injury reports on Kansas appeared to be exaggerated. Therefore, the team was undervalued, significantly increasing the overall parlay payout from $5.10 without Kansas to $12.05 when the Jayhawks are added to the bet. While the overall payout was still modest, all teams were victorious.

Because of the high winning bet percentages for both money lines and spreads for #3 and #4 seeds in the first round (See Table 7), the gambler could have put together numerous two and three team winning team combinations such as Illinois, Baylor, Creighton, Duke, and Kansas, provided the unexpected missteps of Auburn, Marquette, BYU, and Kentucky were avoided.

Example #4 (two-team parlay)

- 737 Oregon Over 150; 770 Florida Over 158

Bet of:	$10	$15	$20	$25	$30	$
Payout:	$26.45	$39.67	$52.89	$66.12	$79.34	

Review of the first round Totals exposed Oregon and Florida as teams likely to score big and not be expected to defend in any exception way. The bet was a winner.

Example #5 (three-team parlay)

- 778 Clemson +2; 770 Florida +1; 771 Utah State +4

Bet of:	$10	$15	$20	$25	$30	$
Payout:	$59.58	$89.37	$119.16	$148.95	$178.74	

This was a calculated deep dive into the typically uncertain high-seed, grey area of the matrix (See page 74). The plan was to pick up a big payout with the spreads on these three dogs all of which had been playing well and were matched with beatable opponents. Colorado didn't get the memo, registering a two-point victory against Florida and making the ticket a loser.

Example #6 (three-team parlay)

- 740 Creighton -11½; 776 Baylor -13½; 773 Longwood +25

Bet of:	$10	$15	$20	$25	$30	$
Payout:	$59.58	$89.37	$119.16	$148.95	$178.74	

On this ticket, the expectation was that Creighton and Baylor would cover but that Houston would not be able to beat Longwood by the required 25 points. The result was that Creighton and Baylor covered. However, although Longwood was only behind by three points at the half, the team ultimately lost by forty points making the parlay a loser.

Example #7 (seven-team parlay)

- 760 Duke -700; 784 Alabama -400; 770 Wisconsin -225; 788 Saint Mary's -225; 790 North Carolina -170; 792 Tennessee -278; 798 Illinois -550

Bet of:	$10	$15	$20	$25	$30	$
Payout:	$66.07	$99.11	$132.14	$165.18	$198.21	

The ticket is a transition between first-round Friday games and second round games on Saturday. Because of Friday losses by Wisconsin and Saint Mary's, the ticket lost, but the three Saturday games involving North Carolina, Tennessee, and Illinois were reloaded on a new ticket where those teams won.

SECOND-ROUND SAMPLE BETS

Example #8 (five-team parlay)

- 790 North Carolina -175; 808 Houston -450; 800 Iowa State -300; 842 Arizona -430; 792 Tennessee -265

Bet of:	$10	$15	$20	$25	$30	$
Payout:	$33.47	$50.21	$66.95	$83.69	$100.42	$.

This five-team parlay was the first reasonable opportunity to use #1 seeds North Carolina and Houston with reasonable odds in combination with #2 seeds Iowa State, Arizona, and Tennessee, which also had attractive odds. The result was a winning ticket.

Example #9 (seven-team parlay)

- 812 Marquette -210; 798 Illinois -475; 834 Baylor-195; North Carolina St. -250; 837 San Diego State -240; 839 Alabama -250; 840 Duke -300

Bet of:	$10	$15	$20	$25	$30	$
Payout:	$90.08	$135.13	$180.17	$225.21	$270.25	$.

This is basically a ticket to get back at teams that were perceived to have registered lucky wins in the first round. This "revenge" ticket was a winning bet.

Example #10 (three-team parlay)

- 799 Washington State +6½; 804 Kansas +4; 826 UConn Over 136

Bet of:	$10	$15	$20	$25	$30	$
Payoff:	$59.58	$89.37	$119.16	$148.95	$178.74	$.

Here, the strategy was to use Washington State as a hedge against Iowa State (See Example #8), take the points on Kansas expected to give Gonzaga trouble, and expect UConn and Northwestern together to post more than 136 points. The bet was a total loss, with Washington and Kansas losing big and the UConn total coming up three points short.

THIRD-ROUND SAMPLE BETS

Example #11 (individual bet)
- 640 Purdue -225

Bet of:	$10	$15	$20	$25	$30	$100
Payoff:	$4.45	$6.67	$8.89	$11.11	$13.33	$44.44

This is a straight bet for the money line for Purdue to take advantage of what looked like a mismatch in the boilermaker's favor. Gonzaga was not their regular imposing self in the regular season and in the prior game had luckily drawn the wounded Kansas. Purdue registered the victory and covered the spread as well.

Example #12 (three-team parlay)

- 638 Arizona -320; 646 Houston -190; 644 Marquette -285

Bet of:	$10	$15	$20	$25	$30	$
Payoff:	$17.06	$25.59	$34.12	$42.65	$51.19	

Shockingly, all three favorites were unable to even win. This is a continuing reminder that wagering on these Tournament games is not guaranteed.

Example #13 (two-team parlay)

- 645 Duke +4; 642 Tennessee -165

Bet of:	$10	$15	$20	$25	$30	$
Payoff:	$20.66	$30.99	$41.32	$51.65	$61.98	

Betting the spread on Duke is a hedge on the Houston money line bet (See example #13). By pairing the Duke bet with the Tennessee money line a two-team parlay resulted in a winning bet.

Example #14 (two-team parlay)

- 637 Clemson +7.5; 634 UConn -600

Bet of:	$10	$15	$20	$25	$30	$
Payoff:	$12.27	$18.41	$24.55	$30.68	$36.82	

Accepting Clemson as a 7½ point dog is a hedge against the money line bet on Arizona. Combining the Clemson leg of the parlay with a highly probable victory by UConn provides an offset to the possibility of an Arizona loss, which in fact happened (see Example #12). The wager won.

FOURTH-ROUND SAMPLE BETS

Example #15 (four-team parlay)

- 634 UConn -8.5; 656 Purdue -3; 654 Alabama -165; 658 Duke-310

Bet of:	$10	$15	$20	$25	$30	$
Payout:	$122.83	$184.25	$245.67	$307.08	$368.50	$.

At this juncture in the Tournament, #1 seeds UConn and Purdue had manageable spreads and, when parlayed with Alabama and Duke, provided an opportunity for a profitable ticket. However, Duke, who was probably only still in the Tournament because of a first-half injury to Houston's best player in the prior game, couldn't find the bottom of the hoop, losing the game and the bet.

Example #16 (two-team parlay)

- 1654 Alabama, under 78; 1658 Duke, under 67

Bet of:	$10	$15	$20	$25	$30	$
Payoff:	$26.45	$39.67	$52.89	$66.12	$79.34	

The lack of scoring and formidable defense by Clemson, combined with difficulty scoring during the early rounds of the Tournament, indicated that a bet on the under in the game made sense. The Tournament performance of Duke and North Carolina State supported a low Total by intermission. The result was a win.

FIFTH-ROUND SAMPLE BETS

Example #17 (individual bet)

- 672 UConn -485

Bet of:	$10	$15	$20	$25	$30	$100
Payoff:	$2.06	$3.09	$4.12	$5.15	$6.19	$20.62

With this straight bet, the pitfalls of points associated with the spread were avoided. The idea was to take advantage of UConn looking like a team that was going to run the table for a second straight championship. The $100 dollar bet that was made only generated $20.62, but this is a 20% return.

Example #18 (three-team parlay)

- 674 Purdue -385; 672 Connecticut -11; South Carolina (NCAA women) -250

Bet of:	$10	$15	$20	$25	$30	$
Payoff:	$23.67	$35.50	$47.34	$59.17	$71.01	

This three-team parlay, combined the money line of Purdue, the less favored semi-final men's Tournament team with the spread on Connecticut, the more heavily favored semi-final team with the money line on the women's NCAA Final game. Betting on the three games together, covering Saturday for the men and Sunday for the women, increased the payout beyond a bet confined only to the two remaining men's contests. The result was a win.

Example #19 (two-team parlay)

- 674 Purdue -385; Iowa (NCAA women) +6

Bet of:	$10	$15	$20	$25	$30	$
Payoff:	$14.05	$21.07	$28.10	$35.12	$42.15	

This is the link of the money line for Purdue in their semi-final game with a hedge bet against the money line of the South Carolina women's team, where Iowa received 6 points as the dog (See Example 18). This is risking the use of the Purdue a second time but is not betting against oneself with respect to the women's game, as both wagers in examples 18 and 19 could win.

In the psychology of betting on the women's game, a factor was the effect of Caitlin Clark's final collegiate game, as this may have influenced the other players on both teams as well as the refereeing of the game. Indeed, early in the game, Clark channeled her inner Michael Jordan, emulating his forceable removal of Brian Shaw before draining a famous jumper when she hurled her defender to the floor, absent any whistle, and adeptly connected for a score on root to her record eighteen-point first quarter. However, the South Carolina team was too much for Iowa in the long run and the bet lost.

<h3 style="text-align:center">CHAMPIONSHIP ROUND SAMPLE BETS</h3>

Example #20 (individual bet)

- 676 UConn -6½

Bet of:	$10	$15	$20	$25	$30	$
Payoff:	$9.09	$13.64	$18.18	$22.73	$27.27	

This was an individual bet, spotting Purdue 6½ points. Even with the player of the year, the Boilermakers had no answer for the most balanced team in college basketball on its way to repeating as the men's collegiate champion and a victory for the gamblers along for the ride.

Example #21 (individual bet)

- 676 U Conn -420

Bet of:	$10	$15	$20	$25	$30	$100
Payoff:	$2.38	$3.57	$4.76	$5.95	$7.14	$23.81

A money line bet on UConn was made just in case the final game did not go as planned, with the Huskies possibly not covering. The insurance was not necessary but the wager did contribute to ending the Tournament on a winning note.

FORMATION OF A TOURNAMENT BRACKET

A tradition of the Tournament is for basketball enthusiasts to try to predict the outcomes of all the games before the Tournament begins by filling out a blank Tournament Bracket. Beating the Odds of March refers to the assembly of your bracket as bralcomy™, the study of the conversion of the lead weight of a blank Tournament Bracket into the pure gold of the selection of winning matchups. In this book, the process has been streamlined with the creation of a new "Express Bracket Matrix Analysis Form™" form that utilizes the matrix concept to allow teams to be selected quickly according to initial seeding and regions (See Figure 9, page 65).

The Express Bracket sheet example below represents the prefect bracket for the 2024 Tournament. With the use of this novel system, a Tournament prediction can be drafted in a fraction of the time it takes to fill out a traditional bracket. Getting this big picture of the Tournament in this manner can aid in crystalizing bet selections. Blank Express Bracket sheets are available in Appendix B on pages 105 and 106.

Figure 9

EXPRESS BRACKET MATRIX ANALYSIS FORM ™
(2024 Tournament Perfect Bracket)

SECOND ROUND

Row	Possible Teams in the Top (T) and Bottom (B) of Each Cell		EAST Regional		WEST Regional		SOUTH Regional		MIDWEST Regional	
1	T	1, 16	T	1	T	1	T	1	T	1
	B	8, 9	B	9	B	9	B	9	B	8
2	T	2, 15	T	2	T	2	T	2	T	2
	B	7, 10	B	7	B	7	B	10	B	7
3	T	3, 14	T	3	T	3	T	3	T	3
	B	6, 11	B	11	B	6	B	11	B	11
4	T	4, 13	T	13	T	4	T	4	T	4
	B	5, 12	B	5	B	12	B	12	B	5

THIRD ROUND

Row	Possible Teams in the Top (T) and Bottom (B) of Each Cell		EAST Regional		WEST Regional		SOUTH Regional		MIDWEST Regional	
1	T	1, 8, 9, 16	T	1	T	1	T	1	T	1
	B	4, 5, 12, 13	B	5	B	4	B	4	B	5
2	T	2, 7, 10, 15	T	2	T	2	T	2	T	2
	B	3, 6, 11, 14	B	3	B	6	B	11	B	3

FOURTH ROUND

Row	Possible Teams in the Top (T) and Bottom (B) of Each Cell		EAST Regional		WEST Regional		SOUTH Regional		MIDWEST Regional	
1	T	1, 4, 5, 8, 9, 12, 13, 16	T	1	T	4	T	4	T	1
	B	2, 3, 6, 7, 10, 11, 14, 15	B	3	B	6	B	11	B	2

FIFTH ROUND

Row	Possible Teams in the Top (T) and Bottom (B) of Each Cell		EAST and WEST Regional		SOUTH and MIDWEST Regional	
1	T	1-16 (any seed is possible)	T	1	T	11
	B	1-16 (any seed is possible)	B	4	B	1

SIXTH ROUND

Row	Possible Teams in the Top (T) and Bottom (B) of Each Cell		EAST or WEST Regional	SOUTH or MIDWEST Regional	WINNER
1	T	1-16 (any seed is possible)	T 1		T: UConn
	B	1-16 (any seed is possible)	B 1		

Seeds that play each other in a Round are in cells with the same color background. The winners in the cells with the same color were matched up as directed by arrows in the next round. The arrow is blue when the cell winner is to occupy the top of the cell in the subsequent round and the arrow is red when the winner is to occupy the bottom of the cell in the following round.

65

MAGNITUDE OF THE ODDS OF MARCH

Tournament pundits like to lecture on the astronomical odds against the prediction of the "perfect" bracket. To begin with, from the gambler's perspective, it needs to be distinguished whether we are talking about the prediction of the winners of all the games or adding the extra requirement of covering the spreads on every contest. Generally, when the perfect bracket is being discussed, we are talking about forecasting the winners of the games. This translates to correct wagers on the money lines of each game. The conclusion that is frequently advanced is that the odds of a perfect prediction of winners is 9 quintillion, expressed as 2^63 or 9,223,372,036,854,775,808. One quintillion is one billion billion.

While this expression is more accurate for correctly predicting the spreads for the games, this proclamation is incorrect for which teams will win the money line because the mathematical concept of "permutations" (don't ask) does not count in analyzing these events and the individual game outcomes are bias, not random statistical events with a 50/50 probability. As an example, in the first round of the Tournament, #1 seeds have only lost to the #16 seeds twice in the history of the Tournament. Therefore, the basic statistical model used to arrive at the 9 quintillion figure is unquestionably in error.

To address this flaw, among other things, the true odds of each game would need to be approximated. The question then becomes how far off is 9 quintillion from the actual Tournament odds. Without becoming a stat freak, the refinement that would be required would probably only reduce the odds a few quintillion but the number still would make the odds of a perfect bracket less likely than winning the average power ball prize. For the gambler's purposes, winning around 66% of bets, particularly if a fair number of parlays are in the mix, should keep you financially ahead. Hopefully, your goal is to have fun and be right on most of your wagers, not get rich.

DON'T FEAR THE DOGS

In the Tournament, every team is on the road. The pressure is huge with a single-elimination format that can shake even the most resolute psyche. The rock feels like a medicine ball on the three-pointer, and the free-throw line is like a firing squad.

Beyond the player anxiety, the presence of so many unsophisticated gamblers in the mix means that the money bet on this Tournament is being placed in a way that is not typical of the average betting situation. Specifically, it is the tendency of Tournament bettors to lean more toward favorites than dogs in wagering. With this understanding, the gambler can take advantage of the House having to artificially respond to unreasonable betting tendencies of novice gamblers.

Taking the above Tournament dynamics into account, do not be too afraid to take points on the dogs when the correct moments present themselves. This is especially true in the middle rounds of the Championship!

EXIT STRATEGY

While it is special experiencing the Tournament at the sportsbook of a casino, the length of the Championship, with the first Four in 2024 slated to start on the 19th of March and concluding on April 8th, likely precludes a hotel stay until a winner is crowned. However, whenever you head for home, on the way out of town, bets can be made on the next Tournament round if the odds have been posted and the sportsbook or its kiosk is open. Winning tickets may be mailed in for payment. This is the last chance to be a winner! See Figure 8, Sample Sportsbook Check for Wagering on the Championship Game, below.

Figure 8

Sample Sportsbook Check for Wagering on the Championship Game

The Document is Printed In Color, Do Not Accept Unless Purple Band Is Present

Caligula Enterprises Services LLC
c/o Caligula Entertainment A/P Dept.
One Appian Way
Las Vegas, NV 89119-4377

56-382/412

CHECK NO: 300392573
DATE: 4/28/24

PAY TO THE ORDER OF Susan Parlay 5183FEDBB826A
P.O. Box 400070
Las Vegas, NV 89140

AMOUNT

***177.77

One Hundred Seventy-Seven Dollars and Seventy-Seven Cents***
Accounts Payable
Money Bank, Shallow Alto, CA

300392573   041203824   6906000413

Authorized Signature

- Have some knowledge of college basketball teams in the Tournament.
- Book hotel accommodations early for the best deal.
- Arrive at the sportsbook early to avoid betting in haste. Sportsbooks frequently close by 9:00 pm. Identify a 24-hour sportsbook, if possible, e.g., South Point in Las Vegas.
- Become familiar with the sportsbook kiosk so that you can place bets without a ticket taker.
- Be aware of the sportsbook's smoking policy.
- Bring a quart or two-liter bottle of water to the sportsbooks. Bartenders are not going to want to serve you water unless it's bottled! It is going to be a long day, so stay hydrated.
- Acquire familiarity with betting terms.
- Understand the matchups of the NCAA four region bracket arrangement.
- Be aware that the first round of the Tournament provides the best opportunity to beat the House because of the sheer volume of information and uncertainty.
- Bring pens and highlighters to the sportsbook.
- Obtain the House wagering sheet. These numbers can be confirmed by looking at the betting board at the sportsbook, usually behind the ticket takers.
- Learn the terminology of placing bets.
- Use the House wagering sheet to adjust or completely assemble a matrix chart for each Tournament Round.
- Employ the betting strategies acquired from this book that work for your gambling style.
- Review player injury reports!!!!
- During a Tournament round played over multiple days, arrange parlay bets without being constrained by when games are played. This increases betting flexibility.
- Test the payout of bets on a parlay calculator to see if you feel that the wager is worth it.
- Avoid the use of a team on too many tickets in any Tournament round. Even "sure things" lose. Don't let a loss by one team ruin the profitability of a Tournament round or your entire trip.
- Have an established wagering limit, and do not bet all your money on the first day of a multi-day vacation.
- Utilize the Matrix Chart and Parlay Building Block Sheet in setting up bet tickets.
- Place bets from a **written** menu (bet sheets). Do not try to wing it at the window!
- Check tickets for accuracy as soon as possible. A common mistake of the House is to replace a money line with a spread on a team. This can be discovered when the ticket payout is significantly higher than your calculation. Insist that mistakes are corrected!
- Ask for drink tickets if the sportsbook provides them when your bets are placed.
- Place bet tickets in a secure place to prevent loss or damage and refer to written representations of the tickets rather than the actual tickets during the course of the games.
- Retain losing tickets to facilitate an accounting of betting success.
- Consider reloading in the face of losses on parlays.
- Have FUN watching the games and winning bets!

NOTES

APPENDIX A

2024 WAGERING PAPERS

This is historical information about the 2024 NCAA Basketball Tournament, which may be helpful in analyzing the 2025 Tournament data as it becomes available.

Documents in this Appendix include:
- 2024 Sample House Generated Bet Sheet, pages 71 and 72
- 2024 Tournament 1st Round Basic Bracket Matrix Chart, page 73
- 2024 Tournament 1st Round Detailed Bracket Matrix Chart, page 74
- 2024 Tournament 2nd Round Bracket Matrix Chart, page 75
- 2024 Tournament 3rd Round Bracket Matrix Chart, page 76
- 2024 Tournament 4th Round Bracket Matrix Chart, page 76
- 2024 Tournament 5th Round Bracket Matrix Chart, page 77
- 2024 Championship Game Matrix Chart, page 78
- 2024 1st Round Parlay Building Block Sheet, pages 79 and 80
- 2024 2nd Round Parlay Building Block Sheet, page 81
- 2024 3rd Round Parlay Building Block Sheet, page 82
- 2024 4th Round Parlay Building Block Sheet, page 82
- 2024 5th Round Parlay Building Block Sheet, page 83
- -2024 6th Round Parlay Building Block Sheet, page 84
- 2024 East Regional and West Regional Bracket Sheet, page 85
- 2024 South Regional and Midwest Regional Bracket Sheet, page 86

The parlay building block sheets show the teams participating in each Tournament round in alphabetical order. No historical notes on the team's projected performance against the odds are provided on these sheets. The gambler does not have to fill out any of the cells of the sheet. Rather, the gambler is encouraged to use the parlay sheet writing in the information that best suits them to help assemble bet sheets.

SAMPLE HOUSE BET SHEET

NCAA BASKETBALL TOURNAMENT First Round

West Region Spectrum Center- Charlotte, NC

Thur Mar 21	725 **Wagner**		+2800	
			133 ½	
11:45 am	726 **N Carolina**	-25	-10000	

Midwest Region Spectrum Center- Charlotte, NC

Thur Mar 21	727 **St. Peter's**		+2000	
			129	
6:20 pm	726 **Tennessee**	-21½	-4800	

West Region Spectrum Center- Charlotte, NC

Thur Mar 21	729 **Michigan St.**	-1	-120	
			130½	
	738 **Miss State**		Even	

Midwest Region Spectrum Center- Charlotte, NC

Thur Mar 21	731 **Colorado State**		+125	
			145	
3:50 pm	732 **Texas**	-2½	-145	

South Region – PPG Paints Arena – Pitts burgh, PA

Thur Mar 21	733 **NC State**		+185	
			145½	
6:40 pm	734 **Texas Tech**	-5	-215	

South Region – PPG Paints Arena – Pitts burgh, PA

Thur Mar 21	735 **Oakland**		+735	
			163	
4:10 pm	736 **Kentucky**	-13½	-1100	

South Region – PPG Paints Arena – Pitts burgh, PA

Thur Mar 21	737 **Oregon**		-105	
			132½	
1:00 pm	738 **S. Carolina**	-1	-115	

South Region – PPG Paints Arena – Pitts burgh, PA

Thur Mar 21	739 **Akron**		+650	
			141	

East Region – CHI Health Center – Omaha, NE

Thur Mar 21	741 **Duquesne**		+350	
			142	
7:00 pm	742 **BYU**	-9 ½	-435	

East Region – CHI Health Center – Omaha, NE

Thur Mar 21	743 **Morehead**		+615	
			148	
12:10 pm	744 **Illinois**	-12	-865	

East Region – CHI Health Center – Omaha, NE

Thur Mar 21	745 **Drake**	-1½	-125	
			138	
7:05 pm	746 **Washington St.**		+105	

East Region – CHI Health Center – Omaha, NE

Thur Mar 21	747 **S, Dakota State**		+1150	
			135 ½	
4:35 pm	748 **Iowa St.**	-16	-2000	

Midwest Region – Delta Center, Salt Lake City, UT

Thur Mar 21	749 **McNeese St.**		+230.	
			150½	
4:25 pm	750 **Gonzaga**	-6	-270	

Midwest Region – Delta Center, Salt Lake City, UT

Thur Mar 21	751 **Samford**		+290	
			154	
6:55 pm	752 **Kansas**	-8	-350	

Midwest Region – Delta Center, Salt Lake City, UT

Thur Mar 21	753 **Nevada**	-1	-115	
			136½	
1:30 pm	754 **Dayton**		-105	

Midwest Region – Delta Center, Salt Lake City, UT

Thur Mar 21	755 **L Beach St.**		+1800	
			161	

Above is an example of a typical legal-size bet sheet displayed across two sheets of letter-size paper. The information is displayed in a manner that does not make it easy to find individual teams and certainly does not facilitate the assembly of well-reasoned parlays. This format places too much emphasis on when games are played but fails to communicate, much less organize the seeding of the teams. Further, the sheet does not even discuss any first half bet options. The short-comings of the average bet sheet are solved by the matrix system exclusively provided in this book (See pages 73 through 78).

First Round (Continued)

7:00 pm	740 **Creighton**	-13	-950	7:00 pm	756 **Arizona**	-20½	-4600
East Region Barclay Center- Brooklyn, NY				West Region – FedEx Forum – Memphis, TN			
Fri Mar 22	757 **Stetson**		+3500	Fri Mar 22	775 **Colgate**		+350
			145½				142
11:45 am	758 **UConn**	-26	-13000	7:00 pm	776 **Baylor**	-9 ½	-435
South Region Barclay Center- Brooklyn, NY				West Region – FedEx Forum – Memphis, TN			
Fri Mar 22	759 **Vermont**		+575	Fri Mar 22	777 **N. Mexico**	-2	+615
			132				148
4:10 pm	760 **Duke**	-12	-800	12:10 pm	778 **Clemson**		+115
South Region Barclay Center- Brooklyn, NY				South Region – FedEx Forum – Memphis, TN			
Fri Mar 22	761 **James Madison**		+195	Fri Mar 22	779 **Texas A&M**		-105
			145				146½
6:40 pm	762 **Wisconsin**	-5 ½	-225	3:50 pm	780 **Nebraska.**	-1	+105
East Region Barclay Center- Brooklyn, NY				East Region – Spokane Veteran Arena – Spokane, WA			
Fri Mar 22	763 **N Western**		+140	Fri Mar 22	781 **Yale**		+625
			141				141
9:15 am	764 **FAU**	-3	-160	1:15 pm	782 **Auburn**	-16	-2000
South Region – PPG Paints Arena – Pitts burgh, PA				West Region – Spokane Veterans Arena, Spokane, WA			
Fri Mar 22	767 **W Kentucky**		+825	Fri Mar 22	783 **Charleston**		+230.
			158				150½
11:00 am	768 **Marquette**	-14½	-1300	4:35 pm	784 **Alabama**	-6	-270
South Region – PPG Paints Arena – Pitts ourgh, PA				East Region – Spokane Veteran Arena – Spokane, WA			
Fri Mar 22	771 **TCU**	-4	-180	Fri Mar 22	785 **UAB**		+220
			151				139½
6:55 pm	772 **Utah State**		+155	6:55 pm	786 **S D State**	-7	-350
South Region – PPG Paints Arena – Pitts ourgh, PA				East Region – Spokane Veteran Arena – Spokane, WA			
Fri Mar 22	773 **Longwood**		+2500	Fri Mar 22	787 **Grand Canyon**		+195
			128				131½
6:20 pm	774 **Houston**	-1	-7800	7:05 pm	788 **St. Mary's**	-5½	-105

<h1 align="center">2024 TOURNAMENT 1ST ROUND BASIC BRACKET MATRIX CHART</h1>

(Team half-time and complete-game scores. Spreads are the actual point differentials)

Seed	East Regional			West Regional			South Regional			Midwest Regional		
1	UConn	52	91	N. Carolina	40	90	Houston	30	86	Purdue	36	78
16	Stetson	19	52	*Wagner*	28	62	Longwood	27	46	*Grambling*	27	50
	Spreads:		(33) [39]	Spreads:		(12) [32]	Spreads:		(-3) [40]	Spreads:		(9) [28]
	Totals:		71; 143	Totals:		68; 152	Totals:		59; 132	Totals:		63; 146
2	Iowa State	40	82	Arizona	41	85	Marquette	36	87	Tennessee	46	83
15	S. Dakota St.	33	65	L. Beach St.	35	65	Western KY	43	69	Saint Peter's	20	49
	Spreads:		(7) [17]	Spreads:		(6) [20]	Spreads:		(-9) [20]	Spreads:		(26) [34]
	Totals:		73; 147	Totals:		76; 150	Totals:		79; 156	Totals:		66; 132
3	Illinois	39	85	Baylor	54	92	Kentucky	35	76	Creighton	39	77
14	Morehead St.	38	69	Colgate	34	67	Oakland	38	80	Akron	34	60
	Spreads:		(1) [16]	Spreads:		(20) [25]	Spreads:		(3) [-4]	Spreads:		(5) [17]
	Totals:		77; 154	Totals:		88; 159	Totals:		73; 156	Totals:		73; 137
4	Auburn	41	76	Alabama	51	109	Duke	34	64	Kansas	48	93
13	Yale	34	78	Charleston	34	96	Vermont	29	47	Samford	38	89
	Spreads:		(7) [-2]	Spreads:		(17) [13]	Spreads:		(5) [17]	Spreads:		(10) [4]
	Totals:		75; 154	Totals:		85; 204	Totals:		63; 111	Totals:		86; 182
5	S.D. State	32	69	Saint Mary's	40	74	Wisconsin	20	61	Gonzaga	48	86
12	UAB	29	65	G. Canyon	23	51	J. Madison	33	72	McNeese St.	25	65
	Spreads:		(3) [4]	Spreads:		(7) [23]	Spreads:		(-13) [-11]	Spreads:		(23) [21]
	Totals:		61; 134	Totals:		63; 125	Totals:		53; 133	Totals:		83; 151
6	BYU	28	67	Clemson	42	77	Texas Tech	33	67	S. Carolina	37	73
11	Duquesne	26	71	New Mexico	28	56	NC State	37	80	Oregon	44	87
	Spreads:		(2) [-4]	Spreads:		(14) [21]	Spreads:		(-4) [-13]	Spreads:		(-7) [-14]
	Totals:		54; 138	Totals:		70; 133	Totals:		70; 147	Totals:		81; 160
7	Washington St	35	76	Dayton	25	63	Florida	42	100	Texas	27	56
10	Drake	31	65	Nevada	34	60	*Colorado*	45	102	*Colorado St.*	11	44
	Spreads:		(4) [11]	Spreads:		(-9) [3]	Spreads:		(-3) [-2]	Spreads:		(16) [12]
	Totals:		66; 141	Totals:		59; 123	Totals:		87; 202	Totals:		38; 100
8	FAU	20	65	Miss St	35	51	Nebraska	44	83	Utah St.	43	88
9	N'Western	19	77	Michigan St.	31	69	Texas A&M	58	98	TCU	37	72
	Spreads:		(-1) [-12]	Spreads:		(4) [-18]	Spreads:		(5) [-15]	Spreads:		(6) [16]
	Totals:		39; 142	Totals:		66; 120	Totals:		102; 181	Totals:		80; 160

Play-in teams Are underlined in red. Total scoring numbers in red indicate the lower seed prevailing for that part of the game.

READING BRACKET MATRIX RESULTS (Matrix Charts below)

The results of the games within the cells for the matrix charts below are noted by a red or green highlight over the specific bet option. A green highlight means that the favorite or the Total over prevailed for the given odds. A red highlight means that the dog won for the given odds. If a result is highlighted in yellow the bet was a push.

OIC-which stands for "Odds Inversion Committee" means that for the complete-game, the higher seeded team was favored to win the game by the House but the NCAA Committee seeding was the correct prediction of the team that would win.

OIH- which stands for "Odds Inversion House" means that for the complete-game, the higher seeded team was favored to win and did do so, contrary to the seeding by the NCAA Committee.

2024 TOURNAMENT 1st ROUND DETAILED BRACKET MATRIX CHART

Seed	East Regional	West Regional	South Regional	Midwest Regional
1	758 UConn -27½; -10000; O 144 ½; H -16½; -2680; O 70	726 N. Carolina -25½; -7850; O 133½; H -14½; -1980; O 63½	774 Houston -25; -8000; O 128; H -15½; -1810; O 59	758 Purdue -21; -10000; O 145; H -16; -1950; O 65½
16	757 Stetson +1800; H +1280 Fri: 11:45 am	725 Wagner +1948; H +1090 Thur: 11:45 am	773 Longwood +1800; H +1005 Fri: 6:20 pm	757 Grambling +1800; H +1075 Fri: 11:00 am
2	748 Iowa State -16; -1410; O 135½; H -9; -610; O 65	756 Arizona -20½; -2800; O 161; H -12; -1280; O 78	756 Marquette -14½; -1300; O 158; H -8½; -530; O 73½	728 Tennessee -21½; -2500; O 129; H -10; -910; O 63½
15	747 S. Dakota St. +850; H +455 Thur: 12:10 pm	755 L. Beach St. +1300; H +820 Thur: 7:00 pm	755 Western KY +825; H +390 Fri: 11:00 am	727 St. Peter's +1300; H +655 Thur: 6:20 pm
3	744 Illinois -12; -865; O 148; H -6; -345; O 69	776 Baylor -13½; -1000; O 138½; H -8; -510; O 66	736 Kentucky -13½; -1100; O 163; H -7; -430; O 77½	740 Creighton -11½; -735; O 141; H -6½; -410; O 67
14	743 Morehead St. +615; H +275 Thur: 12:10 pm	775 Colgate +675; H +380 Fri: 9:40 am	735 Oakland +725; H +330 Thur: 4:10 pm	739 Akron +515; H +315 Thur: 4:35 pm
4	782 Auburn -12½; -900; O 141; H -7; -480; O 65½	784 Alabama -9½; -510; O 173½; H -5; -225; O 81½	760 Duke -12; -800; O 132; H -6½; -360; O 60	752 Kansas -8; -300; O 154; H -4; -220; O 73
13	781 Yale +625; H +360 Fri: 1:15 pm	783 Charleston +400; H +205 Fri: 4:35 pm	759 Vermont +575; H +290 Fri: 4:10 pm	751 Samford +240; H +180 Thur: 6:55 pm
5	786 S. D. State -7; -260; O 139½; H -3½; -195; O 64	788 Saint Mary's -5½; -225; O 131½; H -3; -195; O 60	770 Wisconsin -5½; -225; O 145; H -2½; -170; O 68	750 Gonzaga -6; -270; O 150.5; H -3½; -210; O 70.5
12	785 UAB +220; H +165 Fri: 10:45 am	787 G. Canyon +195; H +165 Fri: 7:05 pm	769 J. Madison +195; H +143 Fri: 6:40 pm	749 McNeese St. +235; H +175 Thur: 4:25 pm
6	742 BYU -9½; -435; O 142; H -5; -280; O 66½	778 Clemson +2; OIC +115; O 152; H +1; +105; O 71	734 Texas Tech -5; -215; O 145½; H -2½; -180; O 68½	738 S. Carolina +2½; OIH +130; O 132½; H +1; +115; O 62
11	741 Duquesne +350; H +230 Thur: 7:00 pm	777 New Mexico -135; H -125 Fri: 12:10 pm	733 NC State +185; H +150 Thur: 6:40 pm	737 Oregon -150; H -135 Thur: 1:00 pm
7	746 Wash. St. +1½; OIH +105; O 138; H +½; +100; O 64½	754 Dayton +1; OIC +105; O 136½; H +½; +100; O 64	770 Florida +1; OIH +100; O 158½; H +½; -105; O 74½	732 Texas -2½; -160; O 145; H -1½; -145; O 67½
10	745 Drake St. -125; H -120 Thur: 7:05 pm	753 Nevada -125; H -120 Thur: 1:30 pm	769 Colorado -120; H -115 Fri: 1:30 pm	731 Colorado St. +135; H +125 Thur: 3:50 pm
8	764 FAU -3; -195; O 141; H -2½; -165; O 66	730 Miss State +1; OIH +105; O 130½; H +½; -105; O 60½	780 Nebraska -1; -105; O 146½; H -½; -110; O 72½	771 Utah St. +4; OIC +155; O 151; H +2; +130; O 70
9	763 N'Western +165; H +140 Fri: 9:15 am	729 Michigan St. -125 H -115 Thur: 9:15 am	779 Texas A&M -115; H -110 Fri: 3:50 pm	772 TCU -180; H -145 Fri: 6:55 pm

Play-in teams are <u>underlined</u> in red.

2024 TOURNAMENT 2nd ROUND BRACKET MATRIX CHART

East Regional	West Regional	South Regional	Midwest Regional
#1 826 UConn -13½; -1500; Over 136 Half: -8; -550; Over 63½ **#9** 825 *Northwestern* +700; H +400 Score: 40 75 Spreads: 17; H 22 *18 58* Totals: 123; H 58 SUN: 6:45 pm	**#1** 790 N. Carolina -4; -175; Over 140 Half: -2; -165; Over 65½ **#9** 789 *Michigan St.* +155; H +140 Score: 40 85 Spreads: 16; H 9 *31 69* Totals: 154; H 71 SAT: 2:30 pm	**#1** 808 Houston -8½; -450; Over 132½ Half: -5.5; -335; Over 61½ **#9** 807 *Texas A&M* +375; H +260 Score: 43 100 Spreads: 5; H 5 *38 95* Totals: 195; H 81 SUN: 5:40 pm	**#1** 832 Purdue -11½; -600; Over 148½ Half: -6; -335; Over 69½ **#8** 809 *Utah State* +430; H +260 Score: 49 106 Spreads: 39; H 16 *33 67* Totals: 173; H 82 SUN: 2:20 pm
#2 800 Iowa State -7½; -300; Over 129 Half: -4½; -260; Over 60½ **#7** 799 *Washington St.* +250; H +210 Score: 33 78 Spreads: 15; H 7 *26 63* Totals: 141; H 59 SAT: 3:15 pm	**#2** 842 Arizona -9; -430; Over 149 Half: -5½; -305; Over 70½ **#7** 841 *Dayton* +350; H +240 Score: 40 78 Spreads: 10; H 7 *33 68* Totals: 146; H 73 SAT: 9:45 am	**#2** 812 Marquette -4½; -210; Over 149 Half: -2½; -175; Over 69 **#10** 811 *Colorado* +175; H +148 Score: 45 81 Spreads: 4; H 11 *34 77* Totals: 158; H 79 SUN: 9:10 am	**#2** 792 Tennessee -6½; -265; Over: 147 Half: -3½; -225; Over 69 **#7** 791 *Texas* +225; H +185 Score: 28 62 Spreads: 4; H 9 *19 58* Totals: 120; H 47 SAT: 5:00 pm
#3 798 Illinois -9½; -475; Over 148 Half: -5½; -305; Over 70 **#11** 797 *Duquenes* +375; H +240 Score: 50 89 Spreads: 26; H 24 26 63 Totals: 152; H 76 SAT: 5:40 pm	**#3** 834 Baylor -4½; -195; Over 145 Half: -2½; -170; Over 67½ **#6** 833 *Clemson* +158; H +143 Score: 25 64 Spread: *-8*; H *-10* *35 72* Totals: 136; H 60 SUN: 3:10 pm	**#14** 846 *Oakland* +5½; +210; Over 146 Half: +3; +170; Over 69 **#11** 796 N. Carolina St. -250; H -205 Score: *29 73* Spreads: 6; H 3 32 79 Totals: 152; H 61 SAT: 4:10 pm	**#3** 794 Creighton -3½; -240; Over 146 Half: -2½; -180; Over 68½ **#11** 793 *Oregon* +200; H +152 Score: 34 86 Spreads: 13; H *-2* *36 73* Totals: 159; H 70 SAT: 6:40 pm
#13 837 *Yale* +5½; +196; Over 129 Half: +3; +158; Over 59½ **#5** 838 San Diego St. -240; H -190 Score: *21 57* Spreads: 28; H 24 45 85 Totals: 142; H 66 SUN: 6:40 pm	**#4** 839 Alabama -6; -250; Over 168½ Half: -3; -195; Over 79 **#12** 840 *Grand Canyon* +210; H +162 Score: 38 72 Spreads: 11; H 8 *30 61* Totals: 68; H 133 SUN: 4:10 pm	**#4** 840 Duke -6; -300; Over 148½ Half: -4; -240; Over 68 **#12** 839 *James Madison* +250; H +190 Score: 47 93 Spreads: 38; H 22 *25 55* Totals: 148; H 72 SUN: 5:40 pm	**#4** 804 *Kansas* +4; OIH +160; Over 127½ Half: +1½; +122; Over 71½ **#5** 803 Gonzaga -180; H -145 Score: *44 68* Spreads: *-21*; H 1 43 89 Totals: 157; H 87 SAT: 12:15 pm

Teams that are underdogs and their scores are in *italics*. Scoring numbers in red *italics* indicate the dog prevailing at that part of the game.

2024 TOURNAMENT 3rd ROUND BRACKET MATRIX CHART 2023

East Regional	West Regional	South Regional	Midwest Regional
#1 634 UConn -12; -900; Over 137 Half: -7; -400; Over 64	**#1** 636 N. Carolina -4½; -210; Over 174½ Half: -2½; -170; Over 83	**#1** 646 Houston -4½; -305; Over 134 Half: -2½; -170; Over 62	**#1** 640 Purdue -4½; -210; Over155½ Half: -2½; -170; Over 74
#5 633 *San Diego St.* +570; H +310 Score: 40 82 Spreads: 9; H 24 *31 52* Totals: 134; H 71 Thur: 4:39 pm	**#4** 635 *Alabama* +175; H +145 Score: 54 87 Spreads: -2; H 8 *46 89* Totals: 176 H 100 Thur: 6:40 pm	**#4** 645 *Duke* +240; H +145 Score: 22 51 Spreads: -3; H -1 *23 54* Totals: 105; H 45 Fri: 2:05 pm	**#5** 639 *Gonzaga* +170; H +145 Score: 40 80 Spreads: 12; H 4 *36 68* Totals: 148; H 76 Fri: 4:40 pm
#2 632 Iowa State -1½; -120; Over 147 Half: -½; -120; Over 68½	**#2** 638 Arizona -7; -315; Over 153½ Half: -3½; -220; Over 72	**#2** 644 Marquette -7½; -320; Over 152 Half: -4; -225; Over 71½	**#2** 642 Tennessee -3½; -170; Over 146½ Half: -1½; -145; Over 69
#3 631 *Illinois* +100; H +100 Score: 26 69 Spreads: -3; H -10 *36 72* Totals: 141; H 62 Thur: 3:09 pm	**#6** 637 *Clemson* +250; H +180 Score: 31 72 Spreads: -5; H -8 *39 77* Totals: 149; H 70 Thur: 4:09 pm	**#11** 643 *N. Carolina St.* +260; H +185 Score: 24 58 Spreads: -9; H -13 *37 67* Totals: 125; H 61 Fri: 6:40 pm	**#3** 641 *Creighton* +145; H +125 Score: 34 82 Spreads: 7; H -1 *35 75* Totals: 157; H 69 Fri 7:09 pm

2024 TOURNAMENT 4TH ROUND BRACKET MATRIX CHART

East Regional	West Regional	South Regional	Midwest Regional
#1 652 UConn -8½; -425; Over 154 Half: -4½; -280; Over 73	**#4** 654 Alabama -3; -165; Over 163½ Half: -2; -150; Over 78	**#4** 658 Duke -7; -310; Over 142 Half: -4; -225 Over 67	**#1** 656 Purdue -3; -170; Over 148 Half: -2; -150 Over 69½
#3 651 *Illinois* +320; H +230 Score: 28 77 Spreads: 25; H 5 *23 52* Totals: 129; H 51 Sat: 3:09 pm	**#6** 653 *Clemson* +135; H +130 Score: 35 89 Spreads: 7; H 3 *32 82* Totals: 171; H 67 Sat: 5:49 pm	**#11** 657 *N. Carolina St.* +255; H +185 Score: 27 64 Spreads: -12; H 6 *21 76* Totals: 140; H 48 Sun: 2:05 pm	**#2** 655 *Tennessee* +145; H +130 Score: 36 72 Spreads: 6; H 2 *34 66* Totals: 138; H 70 Sun: 11:20 am

Teams that are underdogs and their scores are in *italics*. Scoring numbers in red *italics* indicate the dog prevailing at that part of the game.

2024 TOURNAMENT 5TH ROUND BRACKET MATRIX CHART

#1 672 UConn -11½; -650; Over 160½ Half: -6½; -385; Over 60½ **#4** 671 *Alabama* +475; H +300 Score: 44 86 Spreads: 14; H 4 *40 72* Totals: 158; H 84 Sat: 6:20 pm	**#11** 673 *North Carolina State* +9½; +375; Over 145½ Half: +5½; +250; Over 68½ **#1** 674 Purdue -500; H -310 Score: *29 50* Spreads: 7; H 6 35 63 Totals: 113; H 64 Sat: 3:09 pm

Teams that are underdogs and their scores are in *italics*. Scoring numbers in red *italics* indicate the dog prevailing at that part of the game.

2024 CHAMPIONSHIP GAME MATRIX CHART

#1 676 UConn -6½;
-300; Over 145½
Half -3½; -200;
Over 68½
#1 675 *Purdue*
+240; +180

Score:
36 75
Purdue 30 60

Spreads: 15; H 6
Totals: 145.5; H 67

Mon: 6:20 pm

The underdog team score is in italics.

2024 TOURNAMENT 1st ROUND PARLAY BUILDING BLOCK SHEET

#	TEAM; Seed #; Bet #	WIN money Line?	WIN 1st Half ML	COVER GAME SPREAD?	COVER 1st HALF?	GAME Over?	HALF Over?	Play Day	CELL	Opp Line #
1	Akron #14, 739							Thur	4, 4	13
2	Alabama #4, 784							Fri	2, 4	8
3	Arizona #2, 756							Thur	2, 2	30
4	Auburn #4, 782							Fri	1, 4	68
5	Baylor #3, 776							Fri	2, 3	10
6	*Boise State #10, 704*							N/A	N/A	11
7	BYU #6, 742							Thur	1, 6	16
8	Charleston #13, 783							Fri	2, 4	2
9	Clemson #6, 778							Fri	2, 6	40
10	Colgate #14, 775							Fri	2, 3	5
11	**Colorado** #10, 769							Fri	3, 7	18
12	**Colorado St.** #10, 731							Thur	4, 7	56
13	Creighton #3, 740							Thur	4, 3	1
14	Dayton #7, 754							Thur	2, 7	39
15	Duke #4, 760							Fri	3, 4	62
16	Duquesne #11, 741							Thur	1, 6	7
17	Drake #10, 745							Thur	1, 7	65
18	Florida #7, 770							Fri	3, 7	11
19	FL Atlantic #8, 764							Fri	1, 8	43
20	Gonzaga #5, 750							Thur	4, 5	33
21	G. Canyon #12, 787							Fri	2, 5	47
22	**Grambling St.** #16, 757							Fri	4, 1	34,46
23	Houston #1, 774							Fri	3, 1	31
24	*Howard #16, 670*							N/A	N/A	64
25	Illinois #3, 744							Thur	1, 3	35
26	Iowa St. #2, 748							Thur	1, 2	53
27	J. Madison #12, 769							Fri	3, 5	67
28	Kansas #4, 752							Thur	4, 4	49
29	Kentucky #3, 736							Thur	3, 3	44
30	L. Beach St. #15, 755							Thur	2, 2	3
31	Longwood #16, 773							Fri	3, 1	23
32	Marquette #2, 756							Fri	3, 2	66
33	McNeese St. #12, 749							Thur	4, 5	20
34	*Montana St. #16, 702*							N/A	N/A	22
35	Morehead St. #14, 743							Thur	1, 3	25
36	Michigan St. #9, 729							Thur	2, 8	37
37	Mississippi St. #8, 729							Thur	2, 8	36
38	Nebraska #8, 780							Fri	3, 8	57
39	Nevada #10, 753							Thur	2, 7	14

2024 TOURNAMENT 1ST ROUND PARLAY BUILDING BLOCK SHEET (Continued)

#	TEAM; Seed #; Bet #	WIN money Line?	WIN 1st Half Money Line?	COVER GAME SPREAD?	COVER 1st HALF?	GAME Over?	HALF Over?	Play Day	CELL	Opp Line #
40	New Mexico #11, 777							Fri	2, 7	9
41	North Carolina #1, 726							Thur	2, 1	67
42	N. Carolina St. #11, 733							Thur	2, 6	58
43	Northwestern #9, 763							Fri	1, 8	19
44	Oakland #14, 735							Thur	3, 3	29
45	Oregon #11, 737							Thur	4, 6	52
46	Purdue #1, 758							Fri	4, 1	22
47	Saint Mary's #5, 788							Fri	2, 5	21
48	Saint Peter's #15, 727							Thur	4, 2	55
49	Samford #13, 751							Thur	4, 4	28
50	San Diego St. #5, 780							Fri	1, 5	59
51	Stetson #16, 757							Fri	1, 1	60
52	South Carolina #6, 738							Thur	4, 6	45
53	S. Dakota St. #15, 747							Thur	1, 2	26
54	TCU #9, 772							Fri	4, 8	61
55	Tennessee #2, 728							Thur	4, 2	48
56	Texas #7, 732							Thur	3, 6	12
57	Texas A&M #9, 779							Fri	3, 8	38
58	Texas Tech #6, 734							Thur	3, 6	42
59	UAB #12, 785							Fri	1, 5	50
60	UConn #1, 758							Fri	1, 1	51
61	Utah State #8, 771							Fri	4, 8	54
62	Vermont #13, 759							Fri	3, 4	15
63	*Virginia* #10, 672							N/A	N/A	12
64	***Wagner*** #16, 725							Thur	2, 1	24
65	Wash. St. #7, 746							Thur	1, 7	17
66	W. Kentucky #15, 755							Fri	3, 2	32
67	Wisconsin #5, 770							Fri	3, 5	27
68	Yale #13, 781							Fri	1, 4	4

Teams in *italics* are play-in teams. Teams in black italics are the winners of play-in games, with the losers of those games in red italics.

The "CELL" column on the parlay building blocks sheet shows a team's position on the First Round Matrix Chart. The first number is the **column** on the matrix chart, starting from left to right. Thus, the number 4 is the Midwest Regional. The second number is the **row** of the matrix starting from the top.

2024 TOURNAMENT 2nd ROUND PARLAY BUILDING BLOCK SHEET

#	TEAM; Seed #; Bet #	WIN money Line?	WIN 1st Half Money Line?	COVER GAME SPREAD?	COVER 1st HALF?	GAME Over?	HALF Over?	Play Day	CELL	Opp Line #
1	Alabama #4, 839							Sun	2, 4	11
2	Arizona #2, 842							Sat	2, 2	7
3	Baylor #3, 834							Sun	2, 3	4
4	Clemson #6, 833							Sun	2, 3	3
5	Colorado #10, 811							Sun	3, 2	17
6	Creighton #3, 794							Sat	4, 3	23
7	Dayton #7, 841							Sat	2, 2	2
8	Duke #4, 840							Sun	3, 4	15
9	Duquesne #11,							Sat	1, 3	13
10	Gonzaga #5, 803							Sat	1, 4	16
11	G. Canyon #12, 480							Sun	2, 4	1
12	Houston #1, 808							Sun	3, 1	28
13	Illinois #3, 798							Sat	1, 3	9
14	Iowa St. #2, 800							Sat	1, 2	31
15	J. Madison #12, 839							Sun	3, 4	8
16	Kansas #4, 804							Sat	4, 4	10
17	Marquette #2, 812							Sun	3, 2	5
18	Michigan St. #9, 789							Sat	2, 1	19
19	North Carolina #1, 790							Sat	2, 1	18
20	N. Carol. St. #11, 796							Sat	3. 3	22
21	Northwestern #9, 825							Sun	1, 1	29
22	Oakland #14, 846							Sat	3, 3	20
23	Oregon #11, 793							Sat	4, 3	6
24	Purdue #1, 832							Sun	4, 1	30
25	San Diego St. #5, 838							Sun	1, 4	32
26	Tennessee #2, 792							Sat	4, 2	27
27	Texas #7, 791							Sat	4, 2	26
28	Texas A&M #9, 807							Sun	3, 1	12
29	UConn #1. 826							Sun	1, 1	21
30	Utah St. #8, 809							Sun	4, 1	24
31	Washington St. #7, 799							Sat	1, 2	14
32	Yale #13, 837							Sun	1, 4	25

The "CELL" column on the parlay building blocks sheet shows a team's position on the Second Round Matrix Chart. The first number is the **column** on the matrix chart, starting from left to right. Thus, the number 4 is the Midwest. The second number is the **row** of the matrix starting from the top.

#	TEAM; Seed #; Bet #	WIN money Line?	WIN 1st Half Money Line?	COVER GAME SPREAD?	COVER 1st HALF?	GAME Over?	HALF Over?	Play Day	CELL	Opp Line #
1	Alabama #4, 635							Thur	2, 1	11
2	Arizona #2, 638							Thur	2, 2	3
3	Clemson #6, 637							Thur	2, 2	2
4	Creighton #3, 641							Fri	4, 2	15
5	Duke #4, 645							Fri	3, 1	7
6	Gonzaga #5, 639							Fri	4, 1	13
7	Houston #1, 646							Fri	3, 1	5
8	Illinois #3, 631							Thur	1, 2	9
9	Iowa St. #2, 632							Thur	1, 2	8
10	Marquette #2, 644							Fri	3, 2	12
11	North Carolina #1, 636							Thur	2, 1	1
12	N. Carol State #11, 643							Fri	3, 2	10
13	Purdue #1, 640							Fri	4, 1	6
14	San Diego St. #5, 633							Thur	1, 1	16
15	Tennessee #2, 642							Fri	4, 2	4
16	UConn #1, 634							Thur	1, 1	14

#	TEAM; Seed #; Bet #	WIN money Line?	WIN 1st Half Money Line?	COVER GAME SPREAD?	COVER 1st HALF?	GAME Over?	HALF Over?	Play Day	CELL	Opp Line #
1	Alabama #4, 654							Sat	2, 1	2
2	Clemson #6, 653							Sat	2, 1	1
3	Duke #4, 658							Sun	3, 1	5
4	Illinois #3, 651							Sat	1, 1	8
5	N. Carol St. #11, 657							Sun	3, 1	3
6	Purdue #1, 656							Sun	4, 1	7
7	Tennessee #2, 655							Sun	4, 1	6
8	UConn #1, 652							Sat	1, 1	4

The "CELL" column on the parlay building blocks sheet shows a team's position on the corresponding matrix chart. The first number is the **column** on the matrix chart, starting from left to right. Thus, the number 4 is the Midwest. The second number is the **row** of the matrix starting from the top.

2024 TOURNAMENT 5th ROUND PARLAY BUILDING BLOCK SHEET
THE FINAL FOUR

#	TEAM; Seed #; Bet #	WIN money Line?	WIN 1st Half Money Line?	COVER GAME SPREAD?	COVER 1st HALF?	GAME Over?	HALF Over?	Play Day	CELL	Opp Line #
1	Alabama #4, 671							Sat	1, 1	4
2	NC State #11, 675							Sat	2, 1	3
3	Purdue #1, 674							Sat	2, 1	2
4	UConn #1, 672							Sat	1, 1	1

The "CELL" column on the parlay building blocks sheet shows a team's position on the Fifth Round Matrix Chart. The first number is the **column** on the matrix chart, starting from left to right. Thus, the number 4 is the Midwest. The second number is the **row** of the matrix starting from the top.

2024 TOURNAMENT 6th ROUND PARLAY BUILDING BLOCK SHEET
CHAMPIONSHIP GAME

#	TEAM; Seed #; Bet #	WIN money Line?	WIN 1st Half Money Line?	COVER SPREAD?	COVER 1st HALF?	GAME Over?	HALF Over?	Play Day	Opp Line #
1	Purdue #1, 675							Mon	2
2	UConn #1, 676							Mon	1

There is no column/row matrix at this point in the Tournament.

2024 TOURNAMENT BRACKET SHEETS

EAST REGIONAL

1 UConn
16 Stetson
8 FAU
9 Northwestern
5 San Diego St.
12 UAB
4 Auburn
13 Yale
6 BYU
11 Duquesne
3 Illinois
14 Morehead St.
7 Washington St.
10 Drake
2 Iowa State
15 S. Dakota St.

1 UConn
9 N'Western
5 San Diego St.
13 Yale
11 Duquesne
3 Illinois
7 Wash St.
2 Iowa St.

1 UConn
5 San Diego
3 Illinois
2 Iowa St.

1 UConn
3 Illinois

1 UConn

1 UConn

WEST REGIONAL

1 North Carolina
16 Wagner
8 Mississippi St.
9 Michigan St.
5 Saint Mary's
12 Grand Canyon
4 Alabama
13 Charleston
6 Clemson
11 New Mexico
3 Baylor
14 Colgate
7 Dayton
10 Nevada
2 Arizona
15 Long Beach St.

1 N. Carolina
8 Mississippi St.
5 Saint Mary's
4 Alabama
6 Clemson
3 Baylor
7 Dayton
2 Arizona

1 N. Carolina
4 Alabama
6 Clemson
2 Arizona

4 Alabama
6 Clemson

4 Alabama

2024 BRACKET SHEETS (Continued)

SOUTH REGIONAL

1 Houston			
16 Longwood	1 Houston		
8 Nebraska		1 Houston	
9 Texas A&M	9 Texas A&M		
5 Wisconsin			4 Duke
12 J Madison	12 J. Madison		
4 Duke		4 Duke	
13 Vermont	4 Duke		
6 Texas Tech			11 NC State
11 NC State	11 NC State		
3 Kentucky		11 NC State	
14 Oakland	14 Oakland		
7 Florida			11 NC State
10 Colorado	10 Colorado		
2 Marquette		2 Marquette	
15 Western KY	2 Marquette		

Tournament Champion   UConn   1 Purdue

MIDWEST REGIONAL

1 Purdue			
16 Grambling	1 Purdue		
8 Utah State		1 Purdue	
9 TCU	8 Utah State		
5 Gonzaga			1 Purdue
12 McNeese St.	5 Gonzaga		
4 Kansas		5 Gonzaga	
13 Samford	4 Kansas		
6 South Carolina			1 Purdue
11 Oregon	11 Oregon		
3 Creighton		3 Creighton	
14 Akron	3 Creighton		
7 Texas			2 Tennessee
10 Colorado St.	7 Texas		
2 Tennessee		2 Tennessee	
15 Saint Peter's	2 Tennessee		

APPENDIX B

2025 WAGERING PAPERS

These documents are to be filled out by the gambler, starting with the announcement of the Tournament teams on Selection Sunday and progressing until a champion is crowned on April 7, 2025.

Documents in this appendix include:

*Exact regional configuration to be determined on Selection Sunday.

2025 TOURNAMENT 1ST ROUND BASIC BRACKET MATRIX CHART

Seed	Upper Left Regional	Lower Left Regional	Upper Right Regional	Lower Right Regional
1 / 16				
2 / 15				
3 / 14				
4 / 13				
5 / 12				
6 / 11				
7 / 10				
8 / 9				

See Appendix A, page 73, as a template to fill out this form.

2025 TOURNAMENT 1ST ROUND DETAILED BRACKET MATRIX CHART

Seed	Upper Left Regional	Lower Left Regional	Upper Right Regional	Lower Right Regional
1 16				
2 15				
3 14				
4 13				
5 12				
6 11				
7 10				
8 9				

See Appendix A, page 74, as a template to fill out this form.

2025 TOURNAMENT 1st ROUND PARLAY BUILDING BLOCK SHEET

#	TEAM; Seed #; Bet #	WIN Money Line?	WIN 1st Half ML	COVER GAME SPREAD?	COVER 1st HALF?	GAME Over?	HALF Over?	Play Date	CELL	Opp Line #
1										
2										
3										
4										
5										
6										
7										
8										
9										
10										
11										
12										
13										
14										
15										
16										
17										
18										
19										
20										
21										
22										
23										
24										
25										
26										
27										
28										
29										
30										
31										
32										
33										
34										
35										
36										
37										
38										
39										

2025 Tournament 1st Round Parlay Building Block Sheet (continued)

#	TEAM; Seed #; Bet #	WIN Money Line?	WIN 1st Half Money Line?	COVER GAME SPREAD?	COVER 1st HALF?	GAME Over?	HALF Over?	Play Date	C E L L	Opp Line #
40										
41										
43										
44										
45										
46										
47										
48										
49										
50										
51										
52										
53										
54										
55										
56										
57										
58										
59										
60										
61										
62										
63										
64										
65										
66										
67										
68										

The "CELL" column on the parlay building blocks sheet shows a team's position on the 1st Round Detailed Bracket Matrix Chart. The first number is the **column** on the matrix chart, starting from left to right. The second number is the **row** of the matrix, starting from the top to the bottom.

See Appendix A, pages 79 and 80, as a template to fill out this form.

<h1 style="text-align:center">2025 TOURNAMENT 1st ROUND BET SHEET</h1>

- Team #, team name, type of bet, next team(s) if the bet is a parlay
  Example: 774 (Villanova), Over 133 ½; 758 (Auburn), Over 138 ½

Bet of:	$10	$15	$20	$25	$30	$
Payout:	$26.45	$39.67	$52.89	$66.11	$79.34	

-

Bet of:	$10	$15	$20	$25	$30	$
Payout:						

-

Bet of:	$10	$15	$20	$25	$30	$
Payout:						

-

Bet of:	$10	$15	$20	$25	$30	$
Payout:						

-

Bet of:	$10	$15	$20	$25	$30	$
Payout:						

-

Bet of:	$10	$15	$20	$25	$30	$
Payout:						

-

Bet of:	$10	$15	$20	$25	$30	$
Payout:						

-

Bet of:	$10	$15	$20	$25	$30	$
Payout:						

-

Bet of:	$10	$15	$20	$25	$30	$
Payout:						

-

Bet of:	$10	$15	$20	$25	$30	$
Payout:						

2025 TOURNAMENT 2nd ROUND BRACKET MATRIX CHART

Upper Left Regional	Lower Left Regional	Upper Right Regional	Lower Right Regional

See page 75 as a template.

2025 TOURNAMENT 2nd ROUND PARLAY BUILDING BLOCK SHEET

#	TEAM; Seed #; Bet #	WIN Money Line?	WIN 1st Half Money Line?	COVER GAME SPREAD?	COVER 1st HALF?	GAME Over?	HALF Over?	Play Date	CELL	Opp Line #
1										
2										
3										
4										
5										
6										
7										
8										
9										
10										
11										
12										
13										
14										
15										
16										
17										
18										
19										
20										
21										
22										
23										
24										
25										
26										
27										
28										
29										
30										
31										
32										

See Appendix A, page 81, as a template.

The "CELL" column on the parlay building blocks sheet shows a team's position on the 2nd Round Bracket Matrix Chart. The first number is the **column** on the matrix chart, starting from left to right. The second number is the **row** of the matrix, starting from the top to the bottom.

2025 TOURNAMENT 2nd ROUND BET SHEET

- Team #, team name, type of bet, next team(s) if the bet is a parlay
  Example: 774 (Villanova), Over 133½; 758 (Auburn), Over 138 ½

Bet of:	$10	$15	$20	$25	$30	$
Payout:	$26.45	$39.67	$52.89	$66.11	$79.34	

-

Bet of:	$10	$15	$20	$25	$30	$
Payout:						

-

Bet of:	$10	$15	$20	$25	$30	$
Payout:						

-

Bet of:	$10	$15	$20	$25	$30	$
Payout:						

-

Bet of:	$10	$15	$20	$25	$30	$
Payout:						

-

Bet of:	$10	$15	$20	$25	$30	$
Payout:						

-

Bet of:	$10	$15	$20	$25	$30	$
Payout:						

-

Bet of:	$10	$15	$20	$25	$30	$
Payout:						

-

Bet of:	$10	$15	$20	$25	$30	$
Payout:						

-

Bet of:	$10	$15	$20	$25	$30	$
Payout:						

2025 TOURNAMENT 3RD ROUND BRACKET MATRIX CHART

Upper Left Regional	Lower Left Regional	Upper Right Regional	Lower Right Regional

See page 76 as a template.

2025 TOURNAMENT 3rd ROUND PARLAY BUILDING BLOCK SHEET

#	TEAM; Seed #; Bet #	WIN Money Line?	WIN Half Money Line?	COVER Spread?	COVER 1st HALF?	GAME Over?	HALF Over?	Play Date	C E L L	Opp Line #
1										
2										
3										
4										
5										
6										
7										
8										
9										
10										
11										
12										
13										
14										
15										
16										

See Appendix A, page 82, as a template.
The "CELL" column on the parlay building blocks sheet shows a team's position on the matrix chart. The first number is the **column** on the 3rd Round Bracket Matrix Chart, starting from left to right. The second number is the **row** of the matrix starting from the top.

<h1 align="center">2025 TOURNAMENT 3rd ROUND BET SHEET</h1>

- Team #, team name, type of bet, next team(s) if the bet is a parlay
  Example: 774 (Villanova), Over 133½; 758 (Auburn), Over 138 ½

Bet of:	$10	$15	$20	$25	$30	$
Payout:	$26.45	$39.67	$52.89	$66.11	$79.34	

-

Bet of:	$10	$15	$20	$25	$30	$
Payout:						

-

Bet of:	$10	$15	$20	$25	$30	$
Payout:						

-

Bet of:	$10	$15	$20	$25	$30	$
Payout:						

-

Bet of:	$10	$15	$20	$25	$30	$
Payout:						

-

Bet of:	$10	$15	$20	$25	$30	$
Payout:						

-

Bet of:	$10	$15	$20	$25	$30	$
Payout:						

-

Bet of:	$10	$15	$20	$25	$30	$
Payout:						

-

Bet of:	$10	$15	$20	$25	$30	$
Payout:						

-

Bet of:	$10	$15	$20	$25	$30	$
Payout:						

2025 TOURNAMENT 4ᵀᴴ ROUND BRACKET MATRIX CHART

Upper Left Regional	Lower Left Regional	Upper Right Regional	Lower Right Regional

See page 76 as a template.

2025 TOURNAMENT 4ᵀᴴ ROUND PARLAY BUILDING BLOCK SHEET

#	TEAM; Seed #; Bet #	WIN Money Line?	WIN 1st Half Money Line?	COVER GAME SPREAD?	COVER 1st HALF?	GAME Over?	HALF Over?	Play Date	CELL	Opp Line #
1										
2										
3										
4										
5										
6										
7										
8										

See Appendix A, page 82, as a template.

The "CELL" column on the parlay building blocks sheet shows a team's position on the 4ᵀᴴ Round Matrix Chart. The first number is the **column** on the matrix chart, starting from left to right. The second number is the **row** of the matrix, starting from the top to the bottom.

<h1 style="text-align:center">2025 TOURNAMENT 4th ROUND BET SHEET</h1>

- Team #, team name, type of bet, next team(s) if the bet is a parlay
  Example: 774 (Villanova), Over 133½; 758 (Auburn), Over 138 ½

Bet of:	$10	$15	$20	$25	$30	$
Payout:	$26.45	$39.67	$52.89	$66.11	$79.34	

-

Bet of:	$10	$15	$20	$25	$30	$
Payout:						

-

Bet of:	$10	$15	$20	$25	$30	$
Payout:						

-

Bet of:	$10	$15	$20	$25	$30	$
Payout:						

-

Bet of:	$10	$15	$20	$25	$30	$
Payout:						

-

Bet of:	$10	$15	$20	$25	$30	$
Payout:						

-

Bet of:	$10	$15	$20	$25	$30	$
Payout:						

-

Bet of:	$10	$15	$20	$25	$30	$
Payout:						

-

Bet of:	$10	$15	$20	$25	$30	$
Payout:						

2025 TOURNAMENT 5TH ROUND BRACKET MATRIX CHART

<table>
<tr><td>

</td><td></td></tr>
</table>

See page 77 as a template.

2025 TOURNAMENT 5th ROUND PARLAY BUILDING BLOCK SHEET
THE FINAL FOUR

#	TEAM; Seed #; Bet #	WIN money Line?	WIN 1st Half Money Line?	COVER GAME SPREAD?	COVER 1st HALF?	GAME Over?	HALF Over?	Play Date	C E L L	Opp Line #
1										
2										
3										
4										

See Appendix A, page 83, as a template.

The "CELL" column on the parlay building blocks sheet shows a team's position on the 5th Round Bracket Matrix Chart. The first number is the **column** on the matrix chart, starting from left to right. There is only one matrix **row** at this stage of the Tournament.

2025 TOURNAMENT 5ᵗʰ ROUND BET SHEET

- Team #, team name, type of bet, next team(s) if the bet is a parlay
  Example: 774 (Villanova), Over 133½; 758 (Auburn), Over 138 ½

Bet of:	$10	$15	$20	$25	$30	$
Payout:	$26.45	$39.67	$52.89	$66.11	$79.34	

-

Bet of:	$10	$15	$20	$25	$30	$
Payout:						

-

Bet of:	$10	$15	$20	$25	$30	$
Payout:						

-

Bet of:	$10	$15	$20	$25	$30	$
Payout:						

-

Bet of:	$10	$15	$20	$25	$30	$
Payout:						

-

Bet of:	$10	$15	$20	$25	$30	$
Payout:						

-

Bet of:	$10	$15	$20	$25	$30	$
Payout:						

-

Bet of:	$10	$15	$20	$25	$30	$
Payout:						

-

Bet of:	$10	$15	$20	$25	$30	$
Payout:						

-

Bet of:	$10	$15	$20	$25	$30	$
Payout:						

2025 TOURNAMENT CHAMPIONSHIP GAME
MATRIX CHART

See page 78 as a template.

2025 TOURNAMENT 6TH ROUND PARLAY BUILDING BLOCK SHEET
CHAMPIONSHIP GAME

#	TEAM; Seed #; Bet #	WIN money Line?	WIN 1st Half Money Line?	COVER SPREAD?	COVER 1st HALF?	GAME Over	HALF Over	Play Date	Opp Line #
1								Mon	2
2								Mon	1

See Appendix A, page 84, as a template.

2025 TOURNAMENT 6TH ROUND BET SHEET

- Team #, team name, type of bet, next team(s) if the bet is a parlay
  Example: 774 (Villanova), Over 133½; 758 (Auburn), Over 138 ½

Bet of:	$10	$15	$20	$25	$30	$
Payout:	$26.45	$39.67	$52.89	$66.11	$79.34	

-

Bet of:	$10	$15	$20	$25	$30	$
Payout:						

-

Bet of:	$10	$15	$20	$25	$30	$
Payout:						

-

Bet of:	$10	$15	$20	$25	$30	$
Payout:						

-

Bet of:	$10	$15	$20	$25	$30	$
Payout:						

-

Bet of:	$10	$15	$20	$25	$30	$
Payout:						

-

Bet of:	$10	$15	$20	$25	$30	$
Payout:						

-

Bet of:	$10	$15	$20	$25	$30	$
Payout:						

-

Bet of:	$10	$15	$20	$25	$30	$
Payout:						

-

Bet of:	$10	$15	$20	$25	$30	$
Payout:						

EXPRESS BRACKET MATRIX ANALYSIS FORM ™

(Blank Form)

SECOND ROUND

Row	Possible Teams in the Top (T) and Bottom (B) of Each Cell		UPPER Left Regional	LOWER Left Regional	UPPER Right Regional	LOWER Right Regional
1	T	1, 16	T	T	T	T
	B	8, 9	B	B	B	B
2	T	2, 15	T	T	T	T
	B	7, 10	B	B	B	B
3	T	3, 14	T	T	T	T
	B	6, 11	B	B	B	B
4	T	4, 13	T	T	T	T
	B	5, 12	B	B	B	B

THIRD ROUND

Row	Possible Teams in the Top (T) and Bottom (B) of Each Cell		UPPER Left Regional	LOWER Left Regional	UPPER Right Regional	LOWER Right Regional
1	T	1, 8, 9, 16	T	T	T	T
	B	4, 5, 12, 13	B	B	B	B
2	T	2, 7, 10, 15	T	T	T	T
	B	3, 6, 11, 14	B	B	B	B

FOURTH ROUND

Row	Possible Teams in the Top (T) and Bottom (B) of Each Cell		UPPER Left Regional	LOWER Left Regional	UPPER Right Regional	LOWER Right Regional
1	T	1, 4, 5, 8, 9, 12, 13, 16	T	T	T	T
	B	2, 3, 6, 7, 10, 11, 14, 15	B	B	B	B

FIFTH ROUND

Row	Possible Teams in the Top (T) and Bottom (B) of Each Cell		UPPER and LOWER Left Regionals	UPPER and LOWER Right Regionals
1	T	1-16 (any seed is possible)	T	T
	B	1-16 (any seed is possible)	B	B

SIXTH ROUND

Row	Possible Teams in the Top (T) and Bottom (B) of Each Cell		UPPER or LOWER v. UPPER or LOWER Left Regional Right Regional	WINNER
1	T	1-16 (any seed is possible)	T	
	B	1-16 (any seed is possible)	B	T or B:

Seeds that play each other in a Round are in cells with the same color background. The winners of these contests will be matched up as directed by arrows in the next round. The arrow is blue when the cell winner is to occupy the top of the cell in the subsequent Round and the arrow is red when the winner is to occupy the bottom of the cell in the following Round.

EXPRESS BRACKET MATRIX ANALYSIS FORM ™

(Second Chance Blank Form)

SECOND ROUND

Row	Possible Teams in the Top (T) and Bottom (B) of Each Cell	UPPER Left Regional	LOWER Left Regional	UPPER Right Regional	LOWER Right Regional
1	T 1, 16	T	T	T	T
	B 8, 9	B	B	B	B
2	T 2, 15	T	T	T	T
	B 7, 10	B	B	B	B
3	T 3, 14	T	T	T	T
	B 6, 11	B	B	B	B
4	T 4, 13	T	T	T	T
	B 5, 12	B	B	B	B

THIRD ROUND

Row	Possible Teams in the Top (T) and Bottom (B) of Each Cell	UPPER Left Regional	LOWER Left Regional	UPPER Right Regional	LOWER Right Regional
1	T 1, 8, 9, 16	T	T	T	T
	B 4, 5, 12, 13	B	B	B	B
2	T 2, 7, 10, 15	T	T	T	T
	B 3, 6, 11, 14	B	B	B	B

FOURTH ROUND

Row	Possible Teams in the Top (T) and Bottom (B) of Each Cell	UPPER Left Regional	LOWER Left Regional	UPPER Right Regional	LOWER Right Regional
1	T 1, 4, 5, 8, 9, 12, 13, 16	T	T	T	T
	B 2, 3, 6, 7, 10, 11, 14, 15	B	B	B	B

FIFTH ROUND

Row	Possible Teams in the Top (T) and Bottom (B) of Each Cell	UPPER and LOWER Left Regionals	UPPER and LOWER Right Regionals
1	T 1-16 (any seed is possible)	T	T
	B 1-16 (any seed is possible)	B	B

SIXTH ROUND

Row	Possible Teams in the Top (T) and Bottom (B) of Each Cell	UPPER or LOWER v. UPPER or LOWER Left Regional	Right Regional	WINNER
1	T 1-16 (any seed is possible)	T		T or B:
	B 1-16 (any seed is possible)	B		

Seeds that play each other in a Round are in cells with the same color background. The winners of these contests will be matched up as directed by arrows in the next round. The arrow is blue when the cell winner is to occupy the top of the cell in the subsequent Round and the arrow is red when the winner is to occupy the bottom of the cell in the following Round.

2025 BRACKET SHEET

UPPER LEFT REGIONAL

1
16
8
9
5
12
4
13
6
11
3
14
7
10
2
15

LOWER LEFT REGIONAL

1
16
8
9
5
12
4
13
6
11
3
14
7
10
2
15

See page 85 as a template. Exact regional configuration to be determined on Selection Sunday.

UPPER RIGHT REGIONAL

1
16
8
9
5
12
4
13
6
11
3
14
7
10
2
15

LOWER RIGHT REGIONAL

1
16
8
9
5
12
4
13
6
11
3
14
7
10
2
15

See page 86 as a template. Exact regional configuration to be determined on Selection Sunday

2025 TEAM RANKING MATRIX

Rank	Date	Date	Date	Date	Date	Date
1						
2						
3						
4						
5						
6						
7						
8						
9						
10						
11						
12						
13						
14						
15						
16						
17						
18						
19						
20						
21						
22						
23						
24						
25						

See page 7 as a template.

NOTES

I hope that the strategies of this book will be helpful in all your bets on college basketball in general and specifically in beating the Odds of March in the 2025 NCAA Basketball Tournament. To that end, the following semi-random bet is chosen in advance of the official determination of Tournament teams by the NCAA Committee. The three-team wager "pre-pick" that is being offered but in no way guaranteed is:

- South Regional, #12 seed, 1st Half, money line; East Regional, #2 seed, complete-game, money line; East Regional, #7 seed, complete-game, spread.

With the knowledge from this book, the probability of the above dice-selected three-team parlay winning a bet while minimizing a reduction in the payout can be improved. This can be done by changing to the spread on the #12 seed dog, where the team will be receiving points, and switching to the first half money line on the #2 seed to lower the negative odds number on this leg.

The actual teams for this pick, however you arrange them, will be revealed when the 1st Round Detailed Matrix Chart on page 90 is filled out by the gambler after Selection Sunday on March 16, 2025.

All the Best!

Alan B. Sheats